平话金融丛书

Theory and Practice of Non-linear Liquidity Volatility in China's Financial Market

中国金融市场流动性波动：理论与实践

燕汝贞（Yan Ruzhen）◎著

经济管理出版社

ECONOMY & MANAGEMENT PUBLISHING HOUSE

图书在版编目（CIP）数据

中国金融市场流动性波动：理论与实践/燕汝贞著 . —北京：经济管理出版社，2021.5
ISBN 978 - 7 - 5096 - 8008 - 7

Ⅰ.①中… Ⅱ.①燕… Ⅲ.①金融市场—研究—中国 Ⅳ.①F832.5

中国版本图书馆 CIP 数据核字（2021）第 100789 号

组稿编辑：王光艳
责任编辑：高　娅
责任印制：赵亚荣
责任校对：王淑卿

出版发行：经济管理出版社
　　　　　（北京市海淀区北蜂窝 8 号中雅大厦 A 座 11 层　100038）
网　　　址：www. E - mp. com. cn
电　　　话：(010) 51915602
印　　　刷：唐山昊达印刷有限公司
经　　　销：新华书店
开　　　本：720mm×1000mm/16
印　　　张：11. 75
字　　　数：202 千字
版　　　次：2021 年 5 月第 1 版　　2021 年 5 月第 1 次印刷
书　　　号：ISBN 978 - 7 - 5096 - 8008 - 7
定　　　价：68. 00 元

前　言

　　作为金融市场最重要的基本要素之一，流动性是检验市场是否良好运行的重要指标，也反映了金融市场发展的质量。较好的流动性可以促进金融市场稳定、健康、可持续发展；反之，流动性较差或频繁剧烈波动，将会给金融市场带来巨大冲击和负面效应。2015 年，中国证券市场上先后出现了 16 次"千股跌停"和 4 次"千股涨停"剧烈波动情形，这种短时间内大范围跌停或涨停都伴随着流动性的急剧匮乏，并且这种剧烈波动对金融市场的健康可持续发展都造成了巨大危害。因此，研究中国金融市场流动性的异常聚类波动问题具有重要的理论意义和实践价值。

　　目前，有关流动性的研究大都集中在流动性对于资产定价的影响以及流动性与投资者行为关系等领域，对于流动性自身特征的研究较少。事实上，对流动性未来趋势的预测尤为重要。对于投资者而言，如果可以提前准确判断流动性的变化情况，就可以有针对性地及时调整投资策略，降低交易成本，提高投资收益；对于监管层而言，如果对未来流动性变化情况具有较为准确的判断，那么就可以在市场出现极端剧烈波动之前进行及时干预，避免极端波动情况的发生。而要想对流动性未来变化趋势进行准确预测，必须要深刻理解和掌握流动性波动的特征与机理。本书首先根据我国金融市场的发展现状，提出流动性的度量方法，分析流动性的影响因素，并利用多重分形理论、广义 Hurst 指数以及趋势熵维数等方法研究中国"新三板"市场、大盘股市场、股指期货市场以及能源期货市场流动性的波动特征。其次，利用多重分形实现趋势波动分析法研究中国证券市场、股指期货市场等市场流动性波动特征与机理。最后，利用趋势熵维度等模型与方法预测这些市场流动性波动趋势，并证明该预测方法的准确性和有效性。

　　本书可供经济学、管理学等相关学科的高等院校师生以及从事金融市场流动性研究专业人员、证券公司基金经理等使用和参考。在材料收集、数据处理等方面，四川农业大学高伟教授，成都理工大学吴栩副教授、张希、冯茜颖，以及研究生张菁洋、淳正杰、岳定做了大量工作，在此特表感谢！同时，由于笔者水平有限，书中难免有不妥之处，敬请广大读者批评指正！

Contents

Chapter 1   Overview of Financial Market Liquidity in China

1. 1   Liquidity

The extreme financial risk events triggered by the liquidity crisis also emphasized the importance of liquidity from the perspective of practical experience. Since the "stock disaster" in 2015, China's stock market has seen 16 times "thousand shares down limit" and 4 times "thousand shares up limit" rare phenomenon. At the same time, the SSE Composite Index fell from a high of 5, 178 points to 2, 850 points within two months, a drop of 45%, and the situation of the new third board market is also not optimistic. The third board market – making index fell from the highest level of 2,673. 17 points to 1,103. 78 points in four months (April to July 2015), more than 55%. There are liquidity problems behind the market crisis, and the existence of the same liquidity problem will make the market crisis develop into a more serious situation. For another example, on August 16, 2013, during the early trading operation of Everbright Securities, due to the failure of the trading system, more than 30 large – cap stocks were closed to the daily limit within a few minutes, and the Shanghai Composite Index rose by more than 5% in one minute. Afterwards, the Securities Regulatory Commission found that Everbright Securities used more than 7 billion funds to pull many super – large market value stocks to the daily limit in an instant. There are two possible reasons for the rapid increase of these stocks in a short period of time. The sudden influx of fund led to a rapid rise in large – cap stocks; on the other hand, because a large part of the outstanding shares of many large – cap stocks have been illiquid for a long time, the "real" liquidity of such large – cap stocks is relatively poor. The price impact is also larger. Judging from the response to these two market crises, the issue of liquidity is an urgent issue to be solved, and understanding the volatility characteristics of liquidity and predicting the volatility trend of liquidity is an important part of it.

1. 1. 1　Defining the concept of liquidity

The debate on the precise and authoritative definition of liquidity has not stopped. Liquidity can generally be expressed from both macro and micro perspectives. Macro – liquidity, from the national macro level, mainly refers to the money supply of the country's money market, financial market, and the currency stock and supply of commercial banks; Micro – liquidity mainly measures the ability of stocks and other financial assets to convert to cash. The liquidity studied and discussed in this book mainly refers to micro – liquidity.

At present, there are still many disputes on the definition of liquidity in academia. In 1958, Tobin first proposed the concept of financial asset liquidity. He believes: in a transaction, if the seller wants to complete the transaction as soon as possible, then the potential loss is the way to measure the degree of liquidity of the asset. Fisher (1959) defines liquidity as the ability to transfer assets quickly without causing significant loss of value. Demsetz (1968) defines liquidity as the price concession that market participants need to bear in order to successfully complete the transaction. Amihud and Mendelson (1989) believe that liquidity is the cost that investors need to pay if they want to complete the transaction immediately. Massimb and Phelps (1994) define liquidity as the ability to provide immediate execution of transactions for orders in the market, or the ability to execute small market price orders without causing significant changes in the security market prices. O ' Hara (1995) believes that liquidity is the price at which transactions are completed immediately. Chordia et al. (2000) defines liquidity as the ability to buy and sell large amounts of assets quickly at low cost. Liu (2012) believes that the essence of liquidity is the ability of investors to quickly trade a certain amount of assets at a reasonable price based on the basic supply and demand conditions of the market, or the cost to quickly implement a certain amount of transactions.

Many scholars believe that liquidity is a multi – dimensional concept. Black (1971) believes that when any number of orders for a certain security in the market can be bought and sold at any time, then the market has better liquidity. Pastor and Stambaugh (2003) point out that liquidity is the ability to quickly complete a large number of transactions at a lower cost without changing the price of a security. Borio (2004) believes that if transactions in the security market can be completed quickly and have little impact on their prices, then the market has better liquidity. Therefore, the definition of the concept of liquidity needs to be analyzed from different dimensions. Existing studies mainly describe the concept of liquidity from five dimensions:

tightness, depth, breadth, flexibility, and timeliness.

The so - called tightness refers to the size of the implied costs in the transaction process. The implied costs of securities transactions mainly include bid - ask spreads, effective spreads, and realized spreads. Thereinto, the bid - ask spread measures the potential order execution cost; the effective spread reflects the difference between the average price of orders transaction and the midpoint of the bid and ask quotes when the order is reached; the realized spread measures the difference between the order execution price and the midpoint of the bid and ask quotes within a period of time after the order is executed, reflecting the market impact cost after the order is executed. Generally speaking, the smaller the implied cost of order execution, the better the liquidity of the market; Conversely, the greater the implied cost, the worse the liquidity of the market.

Depth is a measure of the quantity that can be traded in the market at a certain price level, and is used to measure the degree of market price stability. If the depth of the market is larger, then the impact of investor orders on the price of securities is smaller; On the contrary, if the depth of the market is smaller, then the impact of investor orders on the price of securities will be greater.

Breadth mainly refers to the complexity of the types of the security market participants. The wider the market, it means that there are more different types of market participants. At this time, the risk of the security market being controlled by very few investors is small, and the market can fully reflect the current supply and demand situation and future market expectation. Judging the breadth of a securities market is mainly from the following perspectives:

(1) There are many different types of investors entering the market at the same time. For example: institutional investors, fund clients, individual investors, long -

term investors and short – term investors, etc.

(2) The purpose of investors participating in the security market transactions is the same. For example: hedging, investment, speculation, etc.

(3) Investors have the same degree of risk preference. For example, risk aversion, risk preference, risk neutrality.

(4) The investment time limit is the same. For example, some investors are short – term transactions and sell in an instant; some investors are long – term holdings and value investments.

The so – called elasticity refers to the speed at which the equilibrium price is restored after a certain number of transactions cause the price to deviate from the equilibrium level. In a highly liquid market measured by elasticity, price will immediately return to an effective level. When the price changes due to temporary order imbalance, a large number of new orders enter the market immediately, the market is elastic; when the order flow adjusts slowly to price changes, then the market is inelastic at this time.

The immediacy mainly refers to the transaction speed or the transaction execution time. Commonly using time method to measure, its advantages are simple method and easy operation. Disadvantages are: the execution time of limit order is closely related to its price, transaction frequency is related to market volatility, and the impact of price changes is not considered. The main indicators of the time method are execution time and transaction frequency. Execution time refers to the interval from the time an order is reached to when the order is executed; Transaction frequency is the number of transactions within a specific time.

1. 1. 2　Liquidity indicators measurement

Although the academic circles have conducted a lot of discussions on the measurement of liquidity, until now, there is still no uniform standard. Regarding the selection of liquidity measurement indicators, scholars also consider from multiple dimensions. Amihud and Mendelson (1986) studied the relationship between the expected rate of return of an asset and its bid－ask spread and found that there is a positive correlation between the two and the bid－ask spread can be used as a measure of liquidity. Kyle (2003) and Hasbrouck (2003) measure liquidity indicators from the depth and width of the market respectively. Amihud (2002) uses the ratio of stock's absolute return to turnover as an indicator of illiquidity and studies the relationship between liquidity and stock returns. The study finds that expected market illiquidity has a positive effect on the excess return of stocks.

Liquidity is a multi－dimensional concept, and effective measurement of liquidity also needs to start from different dimensions. Many scholars have studied the measurement of liquidity from the perspectives of transaction costs and price shocks; some scholars have also proposed measurement indicators suitable for high－frequency trading and low－frequency trading. For high－frequency trading data, the measurement of liquidity can be understood from the perspective of transaction costs. Specific indicators include spreads, market shocks, market depth, transaction volume, and order imbalances. In addition, the degree of information asymmetry will also affect market liquidity. In the extreme case of complete asymmetric information, liquidity providers in the security market will choose to withdraw from trading and no longer provide liquidity to the market. At this time, the security market will suffer from a lack of liquidity. In extreme cases, the entire market will have no more transactions. For example, the daily limit of a certain stock means that all liquidity providers (sellers) of the stock have withdrawn from the transaction, and the stock's liquidity is zero at this time. The main liquidity indicators for informed transactions include: PIN measurement, transaction volume synchronization VPIN measurement, transaction volume weighted VWPIN measurement, and so on. In fact, although liquidity indicators based on high – frequency trading are more accurate, in the actual measurement process, due to the availability and difficulty of calculation of high – frequency trading data, low – frequency trading is used to calculate liquidity in many cases.

To measure liquidity from the perspective of transaction costs (spreads), Roll uses the covariance of the first – order difference time series of stock prices to measure the bid – ask spread; then, Corwin and Stulz use the daily highest and lowest prices to estimate the bid – ask spread; Abdi and Ranaldo use key price indicators such as daily closing price, opening price, highest and lowest prices to measure the bid – ask spread. Goyenko et al. used the transaction data of the US stock market from 1993 to 2005, and used three measurement standards including cross – sectional correlation coefficient, time series correlation coefficient and forecast error to analyze the effectiveness of liquidity measurement indicators such as effective spreads, realized spreads, and price shocks. The study found that low – frequency liquidity indicators such as spreads can better reflect the characteristics of market liquidity, but there is no optimal liquidity measurement indicator at any time, any problem, or under any environment. For investors, the more suitable measurement indicators need to be determined according to specific research issues and the environment.

Regarding the measurement of market shocks, Amihud proposed a well – known illiquidity measurement indicator, in addition, the coefficient, the Amivest current ratio (Amivest indicator) and other measurement indicators. Regarding the Amihud measurement indicator, Fong et al. used historical stock trading data from 42 stock exchanges around the world to study and found that the quoted price spread at the close of each day and the Amihud measurement are the optimal liquidity measurement indicators. Regarding the applicability of different indicators in China's stock market, Liang and Kong studied the Amihud measurement, turnover rate and other liquidity measurement indicators, and the study found that the Amihud indicator measurement results are more accurate than the turnover rate. Zhang et al. studied the applicability of the bid-ask spread measurement indicators in the China's stock market, and found that the pre-closing quoted price spread and effective spread are better than other indicators, and the Amihud measurement is also an optimal measurement indicator. In addition to the bid-ask spread, Wan et al. studied the effectiveness of effective spreads, realized spreads, market depth, and coefficients based on historical Transaction data in China's stock market. The research found that the improved Roll indicator proposed by Kim and Lee is the optimal indicator in width dimension; Transaction volume is the optimal low-frequency indicator in the depth dimension; and the improved Amihud measure proposed by Yang is the optimal indicator in the price shock dimension.

Due to the conflicts among the different dimensions or basic attributes of liquidity, scholars believe that there is no "undisputed and operable definition and measurement of liquidity". Based on the price, quantity, time and other attributes of liquidity, the various methods of measuring liquidity can be divided into five types, namely price method, transaction volume method, price-volume combination method, time method and other methods.

1. 1. 3 Price method

The price method is derived from the tightness dimension of liquidity. The main price indicators are: spread indicators, price improvement indicators, price autocorrelation models, and so on.

Spread indicators mainly include absolute bid – ask spreads, relative bid – ask spreads, absolute effective spreads, relative effective spreads, realized spreads, and so on.

(1) Bid – ask spread. It is the difference between the best selling price and best buying price in the current market. It is mainly used to measure the possible transaction cost of orders. It can also be regarded as market compensation for timely transaction services provided by market makers (O'Hara and George, 1986; Glosten and Harris, 1988).

The bid – ask spread can be divided into absolute bid – ask spread and relative bid – ask spread. The absolute bid – ask spread is the best selling price takes away the best buying price. At the same time, the bid – ask spread generally changes with the stock price. In order to remove the influence of the stock price, the ratio of the absolute bid – ask spread to the average value of the optimal bid – ask price can be used, this is the so – called relative bid – ask spread.

Assuming that $B1$ is the optimal buying price and $A1$ is the optimal selling price, the absolute bid – ask spread (*Spread*) and the relative bid – ask spread (*RSpread*) can be expressed separately as:

$$Spread = A1 - B1 \tag{1.1}$$

$$RSpread = \frac{A1 - B1}{\dfrac{(A1 + B1)}{2}} \tag{1.2}$$

For the market maker market, the bid – ask spread mainly includes three parts: order processing costs, adverse selection costs, and inventory costs.

One is the order processing cost. This part of the cost mainly refers to the labor costs such as traders and the normal operating costs of the trading system. It is the inherent cost of the dealer to match the buyer and the seller to complete the transaction (Roll, 1984). Generally speaking, the order processing cost of the order – driven market is lower than that of the market maker market.

The second is the adverse selection cost. This part of the cost is due to the revision of the expectation of the stock value by the trader (market maker) after the trader with private information submits the order (Brennan and Subrahmanvam, 1996). In the market of market makers, the adverse selection cost is a compensation to market makers who provide liquidity for possible losses in dealing with informed traders who have private information (Copeland and Galai, 1983; Glosten and Milgrom, 1985; Easley and O'Hara, 1987). In the auction market, the cost of adverse selection is a compensation to the liquidity provider (the trader who places the limit order). The cost of adverse selection is usually proportional to the size of the transaction.

The third is the inventory cost. It is the cost paid by market makers for inventory, namely traders need to update their quotations according to the changing situation of the order flow to ensure a stable inventory level (Garman, 1976; Amibud and Mendelson, 1980; Ho and Stoll, 1981).

In the auction market, the order processing cost is usually lower than that in the market maker market. Therefore, the order processing cost factor in the bid – ask spread in the auction market is also lower than that in the market maker market. Roll (1989) conducted a quantitative study on the three elements of the bid – ask spread on the Nasdaq national market. The proportions of each element are: the adverse selection (information) cost is 43%, the inventory cost is 10%, and the order processing cost is 47%. The research of George, Kaul and Nimalendran (1991) shows that the adverse selection cost only accounts for 8% to 13% of the bid – ask spread (at least for small transactions), and the order processing cost is the most important factor in the bid – ask spread.

The bid – ask spread method is simple and easy to implement, easy to understand and use, but because the essence of this method is to measure transaction costs, not liquidity, there are still certain shortcomings in a sense, mainly:

The first is that this method does not account for transactions that are executed outside the bid – ask spread and within the spread, so it may underestimate or overestimate the actual bid – ask spread. For example, large transactions are usually executed outside the quotation (namely higher than the selling quotation or lower than the buying quotation), while transactions with negotiable pricing are usually executed within the quotation (namely lower than the selling quotation or higher than the buying quotation).

The second is that the absolute bid – ask spread does not take into account the price of stocks. Under normal circumstances, the higher the price of stocks, the larger the spread, but the trading of high – priced stocks is not necessarily inactive. Theoretically, the minimum bid – ask spread can be a price up – and – down gear. If there are different price up – and – down gears for stocks with different prices, the price difference for stocks with a larger price up – and – down gear may be larger, but this does not mean that the stock has insufficient liquidity.

(2) Effective spreads. The effective spread reflects the difference between the average price of an order is completed and the midpoint of the bid – ask spread when the order is reached, and its essence is to measure the actual execution cost of the order.

Effective spreads are also divided into absolute effective spreads and relative effective spreads. The absolute effective spread is the difference between the transaction execution price and the midpoint of the bid – ask spread, namely:

$$ESpread = P - M \tag{1.3}$$

The absolute effective spread will change with the change of the stock price. In order to remove the influence of the stock price, the ratio of the absolute effective spread and the transaction execution price to the midpoint of the bid – ask spread can be used. This is the so – called relative effective spread, namely:

$$RESpread = \frac{|P - M|}{M} \tag{1.4}$$

It can be seen from the above expression that the effective spread overcomes the shortcomings of the bid – ask spread to a certain extent.

(3) Realized spreads. The realized spread is a measure of the difference between the transaction price of orders and the average value of the bid – ask prices for a period of time after the order is executed, reflecting an impact on the market after the order is executed. Realized spreads can generally be divided into absolute realized spreads and relative realized spreads. The calculation method is as follows:

$$RSpread = P - M1 \tag{1.5}$$

$$RRSpread = \frac{P - M1}{M1} \tag{1.6}$$

Thereinto, $RSpread$ and $RRSpread$ respectively represent the absolute realized spread and the relative realized spread, P represents the transaction price of the order, $M1$ represents the median value of the bid – ask prices for a period of time after the order is executed, the length of the time is generally 1 minute, 5 minutes, 10 minutes, 30 minutes, and so on.

1. 1. 4 Trading volume indicators

(1) Market Depth. Market depth is the ability of the security market to withstand large transactions without substantial volatilitys in the price of securities, and it is an important indicator of the liquidity of the security market. Market depth indicators are generally divided into quotation depth and amount depth. The so – called quotation depth refers to the number of orders at a specific price. Of course, this specific price can be either the best buying or selling price or other bid – ask prices. Obviously, if the market depth of a certain security is better, it means that the number of orders is larger at the corresponding price level, so there will generally not be large volatilitys in the large – scale transaction of the security. Factors such as stock trading volume, number of outstanding shares, and market value in circulation will all have a certain impact on market depth.

The calculation formula of the depth indicator at the optimal bid – ask price level is as follows:

$$D = \frac{Border - Aorder}{2} \qquad (1.7)$$

Thereinto, D is the market depth of the optimal bid – ask price level, *Border* and *Aorder* respectively represent the order quantity corresponding to the optimal bid – ask price.

In addition to the quotation depth, the amount depth is also an important indicator of the depth indicator. The amount depth is calculated based on the transaction amount, as follows:

$$D_p = \frac{Border \times P_b - Aorder \times P_A}{2} \qquad (1.8)$$

Thereinto, *D* is the market depth of the optimal bid-ask price level, *Border* and *Aorder respectively represent the order quantity corresponding to the optimal bid-ask price.*

Depth indicators are intuitive and easy to judge. However, in the quote-driven markets, market makers are generally unwilling to disclose the total number of transactions at a certain price, so the number at the best quote sometimes cannot truly reflect the full depth of the market.

(2) Deal rate. The deal rate refers to the rate at which orders submitted by an investor complete a transaction in the market. The deal rate can be understood from the following three perspectives: The probability of instant execution, such as MOC mode, buy orders higher than the best selling price, and sell orders lower than the best buying price; probability of all transactions at a given price; the ratio of the transaction volume to the order volume when the order is partially executed.

For limit orders, the deal rate is often determined by the absolute deviation between the price of the limit order and the bid-ask price.

(3) Turnover rate. Turnover rate, also known as trading turnover rate, is an indicator of how long securities are held. The calculation formula of turnover rate is as follows:

$$T = \frac{Order}{Total} \tag{1.9}$$

Thereinto, *Order* represents the order size (trading volume) and *Total* represents the total number of current shares.

If the turnover rate of a security is greater, the liquidity of the security is also greater. The turnover rate index better considers the difference in outstanding stock, but does not consider the impact of changes in securities prices, and price changes are often one of the most important factors to measure liquidity. At the same time, the deal volume or the size of the transaction volume is generally closely related to the volatility of securities, but volatility is an important factor affecting market liquidity.

1.1.5　Combination of volume and price

In terms of liquidity measurement, in view of the insufficiency of price method and transaction volume method, many scholars combine price and transaction volume indicators to set up new liquidity measurement indicators, such as liquidity ratio method, price shock, etc.

The price shock method is mainly to describe the degree of influence of investors' orders on stock prices, avoiding many deficiencies in measuring liquidity simply by the bid – ask spread and transaction volume method. Such methods mainly include the following models: market depth model, Glostern – Harris transaction cost model, Hasbrouck reaction function, Kissell market shock model, Hasbrouck – Foster – Viswanathan transaction cost model.

(1) Kyle market depth model. The Depth of Market model was first proposed by Kyle (1985) . It mainly reflects the impact of net transaction volume (the difference between the transaction volume initiated by the buyer and the transaction volume initiated by the seller) on stock price changes, specifically the slope of the curve composed of price changes and transaction volume.

This model analyzes the impact of net trading volume in a fixed period of time on stock price changes. It not only considers block transactions and series of transactions, but also takes into account the depth index of the bid – ask spread. It is an appropriate index to measure market liquidity. Details as follows:

$$p = \mu + \lambda y \tag{1.10}$$

Thereinto, price p is a linear function of trading volume y, μ is the true value of the security, λ is the regression coefficient, and the sensitivity of price to trading volume. If λ is smaller, the stock price is less sensitive to trading volume, the impact of trading volume on price is smaller, and the higher the market liquidity; conversely, λ is larger, the greater the impact of the transaction volume on the price, and the smaller the market liquidity; D is the market depth, which is the reciprocal of λ, namely $D = \dfrac{1}{\lambda}$.

(2) Glostern – Harris transaction cost model. Glostern and Harris (1988) proposed a liquidity measurement model based on transaction costs:

$$\Delta p_t = \lambda q_t + \phi \ (D_t - D_{t-1}) \ + y_t \tag{1.11}$$

Thereinto, Δp_t is the change in the stock transaction price of No. t transaction; $t - 1$ represents the transaction before No. t transaction; q_t is the volume of No. t transaction and may be positive and negative values. The positive and negative sign mainly indicate the buying and selling direction; D is the trading direction, y_t is a random error term.

(3) Kissell market shock model. Market shock, also known as price shock, refers to the change in stock price caused by the execution of an order by investors (Kissell, 2003). As shown in Figure 1.1, the straight line in the figure represents the impact on the stock price after the investors' orders submit to the market. The dotted line indicates the trend of stock price changes when there is no such order in the market. The size of the price shock is equal to the difference between the stock price when the order is executed and the stock price when the order does not exist in the market. It is generally affected by factors such as order size, market liquidity, volatility, and the trading volume of other investors in the market (Barron and Karpoff, 2004).

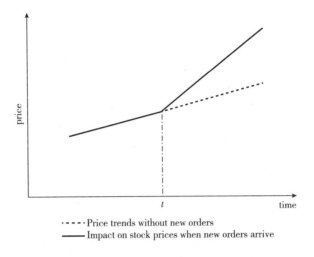

Figure 1. 1　Impact of price shocks on stock prices

Price shocks are one of the most important components of transaction costs. Both academia and industry pay great attention to the research and control of price shocks (Freyre – Sanders et al. , 2004; Dufour and Engle, 2000; Bessembinder, 2003; Holthausen et al. , 1983) . Price shocks can be divided into temporary price impact costs and permanent price impact costs. Thereinto, temporary price shock means that the price change of the security is only caused by the temporary imbalance of supply and demand of the security. After a period of adjustment, the price of the security will return to the original level, as shown in Figure 1. 2.

If the information conveyed by the investor's new order changes the market's expectations for the future price of the security, causing the inherent value of the security to change, then this shock is called a permanent price shock. And this shock has long time impact on the price of the security, and the price of the security will no longer be adjusted to the original price level, as shown in Figure 1. 3.

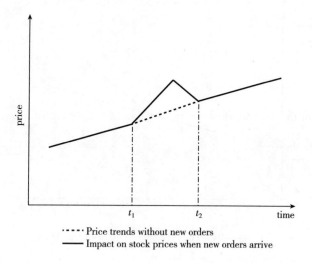

Figure 1. 2　Impact of temporary price shocks on stock prices

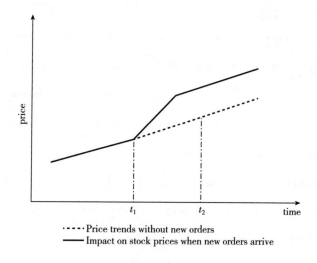

Figure 1. 3　The impact of permanent price shocks on stock prices

Since the cost of price shock is one of the most important components of transaction costs, and it will always make prices change in the opposite direction, investors must study and control the cost of price shocks to reduce transaction costs and increase investment returns. Kissell and Glantz (2003) proposed a method for calculating price shocks. It is assumed that investors plan to use a staged trading strategy to trade S securities over the next m trading period. Thereinto, x_t ($t \in [1, m]$) is the order size of the investor during the t period, the instantaneous impact cost is I[①], let α represents the proportion of the temporary price impact cost to the total price impact cost, and $\alpha \in [0, 1]$, the temporary price impact cost is αI; The permanent price impact cost is $(1 - \alpha) I$. The price impact cost is equal to the sum of the temporary impact cost and the permanent impact cost, which can be expressed as:

$$PI = \alpha I + (1 - \alpha) I \tag{1.12}$$

The temporary and permanent price shocks costs during the t period is:

$$PI_t^{temp} = \frac{\alpha I x_t}{S} \tag{1.13}$$

$$PI_t^{perm} = \frac{(1 - \alpha) I x_t}{S} \tag{1.14}$$

Assume that only liquidity demanders will be affected by temporary price shocks during the entire transaction process. Therefore, the temporary price impact cost of unit securities during the t period is:

$$PI_{t,share}^{temp} = \frac{\alpha x_t I}{v_t^d S} \tag{1.15}$$

Thereinto, v_t^d represents the transaction volume of liquidity demanders during

---

① If investors need to trade X securities for a certain period of time, and adopts a non – split trading strategy, namely all orders are submitted to the security market in the form of market orders for trading at one time, and the impact cost to the investor at this time. It is called the instantaneous impact cost. Kissell and Glantz (2003) proposed the following methods for estimation: $I = a_1 \left(\frac{S}{ADV} \right)^{a_2} \sigma P_0 S$, thereinto, S represents the trading volume; ADV represents the average daily trading volume of the market; σ represents the annual volatility of securities returns; P_0 represents the initial price of securities trading.

the t period.

Permanent price shocks are caused by changes in the price of securities due to the information conveyed by the order itself. When a buy order is submitted to the market for trading, the information conveyed by the buy order will increase the price of the security to a certain extent; If a sell order is submitted to the market for trading, the price of the security will decrease. At the same time, in order to simplify the analysis, it is assumed that the information conveyed by the same size sell order and buy order can exactly offset each other. Therefore, the permanent price impact cost of a unit security in the t period is:

$$PI_{t/share}^{perm} = \frac{(1-\alpha)I}{S} \qquad (1.16)$$

From the above analysis, we can see that the price impact cost of investors who adopt trading strategies x during the entire transaction process is:

$$PI(x) = \sum_{t=1}^{m} x_t \left[\frac{\alpha x_t I}{v_t^d S} + \frac{(1-\alpha)I}{S} \right] \qquad (1.17)$$

The trading volume of liquidity demanders in the t period includes the trading volume of liquidity demanders in the market and investor orders, namely:

$$v_t^d = x_t + 0.5v_t \qquad (1.18)$$

Thereinto, v_t is the total market volume during the t period. Therefore, the above formula can be simplified to:

$$PI(x) = \sum_{t=1}^{m} x_t \frac{\alpha I x_t}{X(x_t + 0.5v_t)} + (1-\alpha)I \qquad (1.19)$$

It can be seen from the above formula that the size of the permanent price shock will not be affected by the trading strategy. The reason is that the cost of the permanent price shock is caused by the information transmitted by the order itself and no matter which trading strategy is adopted.

1. 1. 6   Factors affecting liquidity

Liquidity is very important to both the security market and investors. Better liquidity can promote the healthy development of the security market, and can also significantly increase the rate of return for investors. Analyzing the influencing factors of liquidity is an important prerequisite for improving and enhancing market liquidity. Generally speaking, the main factors affecting market liquidity are as follows: Asset types and asset characteristics, market structure, asset transaction characteristics, market concentration, competition, etc.

(1) Asset types and asset characteristics will have an important impact on liquidity. For example, the risks and returns of assets such as stocks, bonds, and spot assets are significantly different. Therefore, the liquidity of different types of assets is also very different. Compared with the real estate market, the liquidity of the stock market is generally higher; and the liquidity of government bonds is usually higher than that of corporate bonds. Even for the same asset, due to differences in profitability, market concentration, and competition, there may be large differences in their liquidities.

(2) The structure of the security market also has an important impact on liquidity. Generally speaking, the market maker market, namely the quotation – driven market, has better liquidity than the order – driven market; the price of the auction market is more reasonable, but the trading time is generally limited; the continuous trading market has better immediacy. However, trading activity may be poor.

(3) Asset transaction characteristics such as transaction price, order size, and transaction volume also have a greater impact on liquidity. Generally, the larger the transaction price and order size, the worse the liquidity, and the larger the total

market volume, the better the liquidity. Harris (1994) pointed out that low spreads are usually associated with high transaction volumes. The research of Admati and Pfleiderer (1988) also shows that high transaction volume and high return volatility will lead to lower transaction costs. Degryse (1999) pointed out that the bid – ask spreads are directly proportional to the transaction size. The greater the depth, the larger the spreads. The research of Degryse (1999) also found that the effective spread and the transaction scale form a "U" – shaped curve, namely the market impact cost of small and large transactions is larger, while the market impact cost of moderate – scale transactions is smaller.

(4) The type of order has a greater impact on market liquidity. For investors and the security market, there are very different in the liquidity of different types of orders. Market orders focus on immediate execution to complete the transaction; limit orders emphasize the completion of the transaction under conditions such as meet the certain price and quantity; the liquidity of other forms of orders such as limit – to – market orders are also different.

(5) The degree of market concentration also has a greater impact on liquidity. When other conditions remain unchanged, the higher the market concentration, the better the liquidity.

(6) Competition also has a greater impact on liquidity. When other conditions remain unchanged, the higher the degree of effective competition, the greater the liquidity.

In addition, the market environment of the security market, the institutional environment of the security market, the degree of openness, the price limit system, the T + X system, the short selling mechanism, the circuit breaker system, policy factors, and the company's own conditions will all have a certain impact on liquidity.

1. 2   Overview of China's financial market

The so – called financial market refers to the activities in which the supply and demand parties of funds use various financial tools to adjust the surplus of funds in the process of economic operation, and the institutional arrangements for resource alloca- tion of funds, it is the general term for all financial transaction activities. From the perspective of resource allocation, it can be divided into two types: vertical alloca- tion and horizontal allocation. Vertical allocation is mainly about the use of resources allocated by economic entities from different time spans; horizontal allocation is the allocation of resources to different economic entities during a specific period of time. From the perspective of financial intergration, the financial market refers to the general term for the business of currency and fund borrowing, foreign exchange trading, securities trading, bond and stock issuance, and gold and other precious metals trading places.

The classification of financial markets is more complicated. If they are divided according to the financing period, they can be divided into short – term financial markets and long – term financial markets. The short – term financial market is also called the money market, including the bill discount market, the short – term deposit and loan market, the short – term bond market, and the financial institution's inter – bank market. The long – term financial market is also called the capital market, in- cluding the long – term loan market and the securities market. If divided according to the transaction object, it can be divided into the local currency market, foreign exchange market, gold market, securities market, etc. If divided according to the transaction method, it can be divided into direct financial market and indirect financial market. Direct financing refers to the supply and demand parties of fund indirectly complete financial intergration without financial intermediaries; indirect financing mainly refers to the supply and demand parties of fund indirectly complete financial intergration through banks and other financial institutions.

China's capital market was established in the 1990s, marked by the establishment of the Shanghai and Shenzhen stock exchanges. On December 19, 1990, the Shanghai Stock Exchange opened; on July 3, 1991, the Shenzhen Stock Exchange officially opened. Since its establishment, China's capital market has been advancing in reforms and growing in opening up. It has grown from nothing, from small to large, to serve the fundamental purpose of serving the real economy, starting from the reform of serving state – owned enterprises, to the small and medium – sized board, GEM, and the new third board, the science and technology innovation board has been launched one after another, private equity and venture capital have developed in a standardized manner, and the multi – level capital market system has gradually become complete, achieving historic breakthroughs and leapfrog development. By the end of 2020, the size of China's stock and bond markets ranked second in the world, and the volume of commodity futures transactions has ranked the world's forefront for many years; accumulated equity financing for enterprises has reached 21 trillion yuan. Effectively broaden the financing channels for small and medium – sized private enterprises. Since the launch of the Scitech Innovation Board, the amount of IPO financing has accounted for nearly half of the A – shares in the same period; The remaining balance of the bond market is nearly 16 trillion yuan; There are more than 90 types of futures options.

Tracing back to the source, the history of the China's securities market can be traced back to the nineteenth century. After the Opium War in 1840, foreign businessmen began to set up industrial and commercial enterprises in China and tried to issue stocks. In March and April 1865, HSBC established joint – stock bank branches in Hong Kong and Shanghai respectively. In 1872, Li Hongzhang and Sheng Xuanhuai opened the Steamship China Merchants Bureau in Shanghai and began to issue stocks; Until 1882, Shanghai had initially formed a securities market, and there were institutions specializing in stock trading, namely "Pinghuai Stock Companies" and "Association of Stock Brokers". In 1891, foreign merchants opened the Shanghai Stock Office. In 1902, the Qing government established the Shanghai Zhongye Office. In 1911, the 1911 Revolution overthrew the Qing dynasty, and the First World War was underway. All of these promoted the rapid development of Chinese national industry and commerce, the number of joint – stock companies increased and a large number of stocks issued, which contributed to a climax in the history of the development of my country's security market.

In 1914, Shanghai established the Shanghai Stock Commercial Association, which was also the first modern stock exchange operated by the Chinese themselves. In December, the Beiyang government promulgated my country's first securities trading regulations. The stock business association initially had 12 members and then increased to 15. The types of transactions include government bonds, railway bonds, company stocks and foreign exchange, etc. The transaction method is spot trading. The transaction time is 9: 00 – 11: 00 in the morning, and the handling fee is 1% – 5%. The Beijing Stock Exchange was established in 1918. In 1920, the Shanghai Stock Commercial Association was reorganized into the Shanghai Huashang Stock Exchange in accordance with the Securities Exchange Trading Law, which mainly deals in public bonds issued by the Beiyang government. In 1921, the Tianjin Stock Exchange was established. In the autumn of 1921, Shanghai established more than 150 exchanges, many of which also issued shares to establish trust companies. However, they closed down due to the sharp drop in stock prices, which led to a chain reaction, nearly 100 stock exchanges in Shanghai closed down.

The Shanghai Mercantile Stock Exchange resumed business in September 1943; the Shanghai Stock Exchange Co. , Ltd. was established in Shanghai in 1946. As of 1949, there were already four securities markets in China: Hong Kong, Shanghai, Tianjin, and Beiping. On February 1, 1950, the Beijing Stock Exchange was established. In 1952, Tianjin Stock Exchange was merged into Tianjin Investment Company, and Beijing Stock Exchange was also closed. From the 1950s to the 1970s, the securities in Mainland China were government bonds issued by the state and could not be bought, sold or transferred. In the 1980s, the trading of treasury bonds, corporate bonds, and stocks rose again in Mainland China. Taiwan is a part of Chinese territory. The Taiwan authorities promulgated the "Administrative Measures for Securities Dealers" in 1954. In 1960, the Taiwan Securities Regulatory Commission was established and began preparations for the stock exchange. In 1962, the stock exchange officially opened, with 21 companies issuing stocks to the public. In 1967, the weighted index of the Taiwan Stock Exchange was compiled.

The most striking thing from the 1980s to the 1990s was the establishment and development of the Shenzhen and Shanghai securities markets. The Shanghai Stock Exchange was established on November 26, 1990, the Automatic Quotation System (STAQ) was officially completed and put into use in December, and the Shenzhen Stock Exchange began operations on July 3, 1991. In March 2000, the China Securities Regulatory Commission officially implemented the approval procedure for stock issuance. The securities issuance system has thus transitioned from the examination and approval system to the approval system. The shift from the examination and approval system to the approval system is a profound change in the Chinese securities market. It has greatly strengthened the responsibilities of securities companies and various intermediary agencies. It provided a more reasonable institutional prerequisite to improve the transparency of the security market, safeguarded the principle of "three publics", and regulated the issuance and listing of stocks. Improving the quality of listed companies.

The types of securities issued and listed in my country have covered stocks (A shares, B shares, H shares, N shares) and their depositary receipts, securities investment funds (closed – end securities investment funds, listed open – end funds, and trading open – end index funds, open – end securities investment funds), bonds (national bonds, corporate bonds, financial bonds, convertible corporate bonds), warrants (subscription warrants, put warrants), asset – backed securities (special asset income plans, fee – based asset – backed beneficiary certificates), etc.

1. 3   Current status of liquidity research

1. 3. 1   Research on the liquidity of financial markets

Liquidity is not only an important factor in the price changes of securities, but also one of the important indicators reflecting the quality of the securities market. The research on liquidity has a long history, and the concept of liquidity has long been put forward. However, it is difficult for people to give an easy－to－understand and widely recognized definition of liquidity. Scholars usually analyze liquidity from different levels. Tobin (1956) first raised the issue of market liquidity. He believed that when the seller wanted to sell the asset in his hands as soon as possible, the degree of loss incurred could measure the liquidity of the asset. Black (1971) believes that when the market has high liquidity, no matter how many trading orders there are, you can buy and sell at any time. Pastor and Stambaugh (2003) defined liquidity as the ability to quickly complete a large number of transactions at a lower cost without changing the price of securities. Borio (2004) believes that if the transaction can be completed quickly and has a small impact on the price, the market will have better liquidity. Liquidity not only reflects the quality of the market operating environment, but also affects asset returns. For market transactions, investors hope to execute their own trading orders in a timely manner, but if the liquidity of stocks decreases, investors' transaction costs will continue to increase. For such products with less liquidity, investors often required higher returns to make up for losses arising from increased transaction costs. In terms of market supervision, regulators can judge whether the market is functioning well through changes in liquidity. If liquidity continues to deteriorate, regulators can promptly adopt macro－control to avoid the occurrence of a "liquidity stampede crisis". Regardless of whether it is considered from the perspective of market transactions or market supervision, how to effectively measure the size of liquidity is an important financial issue. However, since the concept of liquidity itself does not have a unified definition, scholars also proposed methods for measuring the size of liquidity from different perspectives. Overall, the liquidity index can be explained from four aspects: breadth, depth, timeliness and flexibility. Market width is the difference between the price signed by buyers and sellers and the effective market price. The main measurement indicators are: bid – ask spread and effective spread, etc.; Market depth is the largest transaction volume that can be reached by both parties under the condition that the current price is not affected, the main indicators are: Kyle (1985) depth indicator, Glostern – Harris (1988) indicator, deal rate and turnover rate, etc.; Transaction timeliness refers to the time required for a certain number of market transactions, such as Lippman and McCall (1986) proposed trading frequency and other indicators; Market elasticity refers to the disappearance of price volatilitys caused by transaction. In addition, there are some indicators for measuring liquidity that take multiple aspects into consideration. For example, Amihud and Mendelson (1986) studied the relationship between the expected rate of return of the asset and its bid – ask spread and found that there is a positive correlation between the two. The bid – ask spread can be used as a measure of liquidity. Kyle and Hasbrouck (2003) measure liquidity indicators from the depth and width of the market respectively. Amihud (2002) uses the ratio of stock's absolute return to turnover as an indicator of illiquidity and studies the relationship between liquidity and stock returns. The study finds that expected market illiquidity has a positive effect on the excess return of stocks.

In addition to measuring the size of liquidity, the research value of liquidity is also reflected in other aspects. Some scholars have studied the role of liquidity in asset pricing (Amihud and Mendelson, 1986; Chordia et al., 2000; Amihud et al., 2013; Kelly and Jiang, 2014), and some scholars have studied the impact of liquidity on investor behavior (Chordia et al., 2011; Jotikasthira et al., 2012; Kaniel et al., 2012) and the correlation between liquidity and market efficiency (Chordia et al., 2008; Chung and Hrazdil, 2010). Although these studies have proved from different aspects that liquidity has important research value for the entire financial market, the characteristics of liquidity itself have always been a problem that plagues scholars, so that it is impossible to accurately identify the volatility trend of liquidity. In addition, the efficient market hypothesis has important value in traditional financial theories. The hypothesis believes that the trend of stock prices can reflect all valuable information in a timely and effective manner. However, in the actual operation process, investors are often swayed by market information, and market information will also stimulate liquidity volatilitys, which will result in changes in actual transaction costs. This situation makes stock price trends unable to fully reflect market information. Therefore, the actual stock market does not meet the conditions of the efficient market hypothesis, and some market anomalies have also appeared in the financial market. These market anomalies are an important basis for the failure of the efficient market hypothesis. With the deepening of research, Korajczyk and Sadka (2004), Avramov et al. (2006) and Asness et al. (2013) found that liquidity volatilitys are one of the important reasons for various market anomalies.

The cost of liquidity in the financial market:

Traditional investment theory assumes that the financial market has perfect liquidity, and any order submitted by investors can be executed without liquidity costs. Therefore, investors only need to pay attention to how to construct the optimal investment portfolio in different market. However, in the actual securities market, affected by the limited liquidity of the market (Hasbrouck, 2007; Flood, 1991), orders submitted by investors may incur large liquidity costs during the execution process, especially price impacts cost. If the transaction cost is too high, then the investor's investment income may be lower than the expected value. Florackis (2011), Kissell and Liet (2011), Leshik and Cralle (2011) pointed out that the cost of liquidity is the most important component of the total transaction cost of investors, and the price shock is one of the most important components of liquidity costs, so investors must pay attention to the research and control of transaction costs, especially the cost of price shocks.

In order to estimate the cost of price shocks, Kyle (1985) derives that under the framework of rational expectations, the effect of market predictable trading volume on security price changes is a linear relationship, and uses the regression coefficient of trading volume and price changes to describe the degree of price shock, some scholars also call this coefficient as price shock coefficient. Glostern and Harris (1988) considered the impact of transaction volume with transaction direction on price changes, and believed that there is a positive relationship between price changes and transaction volume with signs. Lillo et al. (2003) constructed a price shock function, pointing out that price shocks have a positive correlation with the market's trading volume, and a negative correlation with market liquidity. In addition, Sornette et al. (2002) believe that the impact of order imbalance on security prices is a linear impact process. Furthermore, Chen et al. (2010) constructed a model of the impact of order gaps and changes in market trading volume on prices, and believed that the order gaps, changes in total market trading volume, and changes in securities prices are all positively correlated. Alzahrani et al. (2013) and Ryu (2013) respectively studied the cost of price shocks in the Saudi securities market and South Korea's futures market, and the results showed that there is a positive correlation between the order size and the cost of price shocks. Huberman and Stanzl (2004), Almgren et al. (2005) theoretically proved that the relationship between the cost of permanent price shocks and transaction volume is linear, while the relationship between temporary price shocks and transaction volume can be Linear or non – linear.

For a specific investment, when a certain trading strategy needs to be executed, not only the impact of market trading volume on changes in securities prices needs to be estimated, but also the additional impact cost caused by one's own orders on the market needs to be considered. In fact, from the perspective of trading strategy, the real price shock refers to the change in the security price caused by the execution of an investor's order (Kissell and Glantz, 2003; Keim, 2003). For a buy order, the size of the price impact cost is equal to the difference between the execution price of the order and the security price when the order does not exist in the market. However, in the real market, since these two prices cannot exist at the same time, when calculating the cost of price shocks, many scholars propose to use the difference between the deal price of an order and a certain benchmark price (depicting the security price when the order does not exist in the market) to measure the price shocks. For example, yesterday's closing price (Kogan, 2006), the average of the highest and lowest prices of securities on the trading day (Blum et al., 1986), the average value of the highest, lowest, opening, and closing prices of securities on the trading day (Domowitz et al., 2001) and so on. However, the use of the security price at one or several special moments as the benchmark price does not reflect all the transaction information of the security during the entire trading period. In order to solve this problem, Berkowitz and Logue (1988) proposed a new benchmark price – Volume Weighted Average Price (VWAP), and used the difference between the execution price of the order and the VWAP benchmark price to measure price shocks. The so – called VWAP benchmark price takes the ratio of the transaction volume in a certain period to the total transaction volume as the weight, and performs a weighted average of the transaction price during the entire transaction period. Although many scholars often use the VWAP benchmark price when calculating price shocks, the existing literature does not provide a theoretical basis for the rationality of this benchmark price.

In the process of implementing investment decisions, even if investors face the same market environment, there may still be a certain difference in the price shocks caused by the investor's buy order and the buy order on the market (Keim and Madhavan, 1996; Ahn and Kang, 2010; Han et al., 2012; Ryu, 2012; Obizhaeva and Wang, 2013). Hu (2009) believes that the main reason for this difference may be that different benchmark prices are used when calculating price shocks, which leads to the difference in calculating the price shocks of buying and selling orders of investors; while some other scholars believe that this difference is mainly caused by factors such as total market volume, order imbalance, information, and the degree of development of the security market (Alzahrani, 2012; Han, 2012; Kang and Ryu, 2010; Holthausen et al., 1990; Ryu, 2012; Hopman, 2007).

In order to reduce the cost of price shocks, most investors will split large orders into multiple small and medium - sized sub - orders, and use limit orders to submit orders one by one. Obviously, this trading method increases the total execution time of orders; At the same time, due to the high uncertainty of security prices in the security market, the order submission strategy formulated in advance by investors does not guarantee that all orders can be completed on time at each stage. In fact, according to a study on the Tel Aviv Stock Exchange by Alam and Tkatch (2007), only about 48% of orders in the market can be fully filled. The loss to investors caused by the failure to execute all orders is called opportunity cost. Opportunity cost will be a factor that cannot be ignored in the process of securities trading (Wagner and Edwards). However, many documents currently use the VWAP benchmark price when calculating price shocks, but they do not give the corresponding theoretical basis, and they do not analyze the measurement of price shocks and the main influencing factors in combination with the characteristics of my country's securities market.

1.3.2　Research on the characteristics of liquidity volatilitys

Traditional finance theory believes that the market is a normal independent and identical distribution and follows a random walk (Fama, 1970; Malkiel, 2003). However, historical data shows that the changes in stock prices do not follow a strict random walk process, but have certain relevance and can be predicted by models. This shows that there is a certain deviation in the use of traditional financial theories to explain the stock price volatilitys in the securities market. At the same time, the securities market often has the characteristics of multiple causal feedback loops, information asymmetry, and irreversibility (Yin and Hua, 2017). These performance characteristics indicate that the security market does not meet the conditions of the efficient market hypothesis, and that the security market often has more complex nonlinear characteristics. With the development of fractal theory, Peters (1991) proposed the fractal market theory. The fractal market theory uses a nonlinear model, which is mainly used to pay attention to the nonlinear characteristics of time series such as long memory and self – similarity. Many scholars have also conducted in – depth research on this, and used the fractal market theory to study the stock market from different angles. The research found that the stock market has obvious fractal characteristics such as long memory and self – similarity, and it has very complex nonlinear structure (Fan, 2004; Huang et al., 2009; Wu, 2007; Xie et al., 2010; Yang, 2002). Yin and Hua (2017) use a single parameter to describe the fractal characteristics of time series at different time points or different measurement scales, verifying the fractal and dimension characteristics of liquidity in the China's stock market, and provide a new idea for exploring the microstructure of the stock market. However, the single – fractal structure model they adopted can only explain the scaling invariance of time series, and the security market has obvious scale transition characteristics in most cases, and this single – fractal structure is only aimed at research on a certain aspect of liquidity changes of the securities market, this likely leads to the loss of many important information. Obviously, single fractal cannot accurately describe the real situation of the stock market, and multifractal theory is a new direction in the development of fractal theory. The introduction of multifractal is particularly important. It can more accurately and comprehensively describe the nonlinear characteristics of the security market liquidity. It can also solve the problem of market liquidity transition in different time scales, and it is an effective method to study the nonlinear characteristics of the security market liquidity. In order to further study the fractal characteristics of time series, Peng et al. (1994) proposed the detrend volatility analysis (DFA), which is used to analyze the long correlation of non – stationary time series. It is also the most commonly used to study the single fractal characteristics of time series. Methods. Although the DFA can explain the long correlation of time series, this method cannot be used to describe the multi – scale and fractal subsets of time series. Later, Wei (2011), Zhou (2013) and Wang et al. (2009) confirmed that the financial market has not only fractal characteristics but also multi – fractal characteristics.

The so – called multifractal is an infinite set composed of multiple scales based on the fractal structure to describe the characteristics of each subset under different scales. At present, multifractal theory is mainly used to study the return rate of market and stock price index. Aiming at the problem of different time scales of time series data, Kantelhardt et al. (2002) proposed a non – stationary time series multifractal representation method based on DFA—multi – fractal detrended volatility analysis

（MF – DFA）. This method can determine the multifractal scale of time series, and distinguish the multifractal of long – term correlation and multifractal of generalized probability density functions. Ho （2003） and Sun et al. （2001） studied the fractal characteristics of the market through the Taiwan Price Index and the Hong Kong Hang Seng Index respectively, and found that this index has obvious multifractal characteristics. In addition, Hiroaki （2002） and Budaev （2004） found that the stock markets of Japan and Russia also have obvious multifractal characteristics. Regarding the multifractal research of the domestic market, Zhao Wei （2007） uses the method of multifractal statistical physics to analyze the high – frequency data of the Shanghai Stock Exchange. The important parameters of the multifractal spectrum can reflect the information of stock prices and related trends but are not applicable for the prediction of price volatilitys, the study found that the time series of the Chinese stock market exhibits the characteristics of multifractal; Du Guoxiong （2007） uses three multifractal analysis methods including the partition function analysis method, the singularity spectrum analysis method and the multi – fractal detrended volatility analysis to study the multifractal characteristics of the Shanghai Composite Index, it is found that the multifractal shape of the Shanghai Composite Index does not change with the time scale, and as the order increases, the generalized Hurst exponent gradually decreases, and the degree of multifractal gradually increases. The singular spectrum curve is getting rougher and rougher; Li Hongquan et al. （2008） found that China's stock market volatility has its inherent nonlinear dynamics formation mechanism, which has the characteristics of long – term memory and low – dimensional chaos, revealing the positive feedback mechanism in the market, the heterogeneity of investors and mutual influence of investors will trigger complex market behaviors; Yuan et al. （2009） used MF – DFA to study the Shanghai and Shenzhen stock indexes and found that both the Shanghai Stock Index and the Shenzhen Component Index have significant multifractal characteristics. Zhuang et al. (2015) used the two dimensions of space and time to analyze the fractal characteristics of China's stock market under the complex network structure. From a space perspective, it proved that the complex network of China's stock market has space fractal characteristics and its fractal dimension is inversely proportional to the network threshold. From time perspective, it proves that the time series of the aggregation coefficient of the complex network of China's stock market has long memory and durability. In order to describe the liquidity characteristics of China's stock market more accurately, this paper uses MF – DFA to study the liquidity multifractal characteristics of China's large, medium and small cap markets and the New Third Board market and compares the differences in the liquidity multifractal characteristics of the three markets.

1. 3. 3   Research on liquidity trend prediction

In the real market, investors and regulators not only pay attention to the liquidity characteristics of the financial market, but also pay attention to the volatility trend of market liquidity. Only by understanding the characteristics of liquidity can the volatility trend of liquidity be effectively predicted. Market liquidity trend prediction can not only reduce investors' transaction costs, but also warn of extreme changes in market liquidity. However, due to the non – linear characteristics of financial markets, market changes often do not follow the conditions of the efficient market hypothesis and do not conform to the characteristics of normal distribution. Therefore, when studying market volatilitys, many scholars divide them into two categories, one is that the volatility direction of the financial market is consistent with that of the previous moment (Jegadeesh and Titman, 1993); the other is that the volatility direction of the financial market reverses (Debond, 1985), which are called volatility trend consistency and trend contrarian respectively. Whether stock price volatility is trend consistency or trend contrarian is still debated in academia (Nnadi and Tanna, 2015; Khan and Rabbani, 2017), Griffin (2003) and Moskowitz et al. (2012) found that the direction of market volatility is maintain the state of the trend in the previous period, with trend consistency, and Lee (2000) proved that market volatility has trend contrarian. Later, Bernstein (1993) combined the two volatility characteristics and put forward the concept of momentum life cycle and analyze the transformation relationship between two volatility characteristics. Galariotis (2014), Adam et al. (2016), Wu and Wang (2016) and other scholars have proved that there is a transformation relationship between trend consistency and trend contrarian in the stock market. At the same time, aiming at the nonlinear characteristics and complex structure of the futures market, it is not accurate to use simple autocorrelation analysis to study the volatility trend of futures liquidity. Mandelbrot (1999) and Xu (2011) believe that it is more realistic to construct a measurement of volatility trend recognition with nonlinear characteristics. Falconer (2003) proposed the entropy dimension based on the nonlinear theory, and used the entropy dimension to describe the volatility trend of time series. Then, Yan (2017) and Wu et al. (2018) used the trendrncy entropy dimension to effectively recognize the volatility trend of the stock market. Trendency entropy dimension is an improvement on the basis of entropy dimension recognition method, which can not only recognize the volatility characteristics of time series, but also recognize the direction of volatility trend.

Chapter 2   Liquidity and Fractals Theory

2. 1   Liquidity theory

2. 1. 1   Inventory model

In the inventory model, the market – maker is generally regarded as a market in-termediary. Market – makers resolve the contradiction between supply and demand by offering and selling prices. There is an imbalance in the stock market due to the random buy and sell orders. To solve this problem, market makers must hold certain positions in stocks and cash. The bid – ask spread is based on the cost to market makers of holding these inventory positions.

Inventory models can be divided into three categories according to their stages of development.

(1) The first type of inventory model is represented by Garman (1976) . This

type of inventory model mainly analyzes the nature of the order flow and the impact on the formation of securities transaction prices. Assuming that the emergence of all orders in the market is a random process that obeys the Poisson distribution, a "time – based microstructure" model describing the asset market is proposed.

On the basis of this assumption, Garman analyzed the impact of the Poisson process order flow on the price and the clearing method of the entire securities market. Garman assumed that there was only one monopolistic market maker in the market, and market makers have two goals. One is to avoid bankruptcy, and the other is to maximize the expected return. However, market makers cannot conduct transactions. The only action they can take is to set reasonable buying and selling quotations, and they can only do so at the beginning of the transaction. The action is to set a reasonable buying and selling price at the beginning of the transaction, only one – time bid and purchase quotations can be set. Since the flow of buying and selling orders obeys independent poisson stochastic processes, there may be an imbalance. This imbalance is a key to market maker pricing. Through the analysis of the model, Garman found that under the premise of risk neutrality, the market maker's approach is to set different buying and selling quotations. Obviously, the selling quotation must exceed the buying quotation to maximize the return. The bid – ask spread is a necessary condition for market makers to make profits. In this sense, it can be said that the microstructure of the stock market determines the price behavior of the stock market.

(2) The second type of inventory model is represented by Stoll (Stoll, 1978) . This type of model focuses on the analysis of market makers' decision – making optimization problems to examine the impact of transaction costs and inventory costs on securities market prices. Since the market maker sets the buying and selling price of securities, this behavior of the market maker can be regarded as a process of selecting

the optimal pricing strategy to maximize the utility. Therefore, the quotation in the market is the optimal behavior of the market maker.

Stoll believes that market makers should be risk – averse, not risk – neutral. Therefore, when market makers provide services, they must inevitably need risk compensation. The bid – ask spread is the risk compensation borne by market makers.

The Stewart model is a two – cycle model. The market maker sets the bid – ask spread in the first time period and liquidates in the second time period. The financing ability of market maker is not restricted, and there is no risk of bankruptcy.

We solve the optimal decision problem of market maker, find that the market maker's inventory position only affects the buying and selling prices, but not the size of the spread. The disadvantage of this model is that it only considers one cycle, and does not consider the situation of multiple cycles. However, for an uncertain market in reality, the order flow is uncertain, and it is impossible to determine when the market maker will liquidate. Huo and Stoll further extended this single – period model to multiple periods, arguing that market maker spread depends on the trading cycle. If the cycle is longer, the spread will be greater. The extent of the spread depends on factors such as the market maker's risk aversion coefficient, transaction size, etc. The bid – ask spread is not affected by the inventory level.

(3) The third type of inventory model is represented by Stoll (1983). Inventory models only analyze the behavior of one market maker. This type of model focuses on analyzing the impact of multiple market makers on the price of securities. The previous inventory model believed that the market maker was risk – neutral, and there was only one market maker. In reality, many markets have multiple market makers, the expectation of the inventory position and the behavior of other market makers will affect the bid – ask quotations and bid – ask spreads set by the market makers.

2. 1. 2　Information model

The empirical test results of the inventory model show that the inventory model's ability to explain market prices is very limited. Information models have developed rapidly and have gradually become an important issue in academic research.

The information model believes that the bid – ask spread is not due to inventory costs, but information asymmetry. Even in a market with no friction and perfect competition, the bid – ask spread will still exist. The main advantages of the information model: it can investigate the information transmission and price adjustment process in the market; it can derive the trading strategies of informed traders and uninformed traders. There are two main types of market maker pricing strategies in the information model:

(1) Glosten – Milgrom sequential trading model. Glosten and Milgrom introduced dynamic factors into the information model. Order flow is the medium of information transmission. Market makers obtain information by analyzing the order flow and set quotations. The information models have epoch – making significance in the history of microstructure theory in securities market. Hence, the research focus of market microstructure theory has shifted to the dynamic learning process of market makers.

Glosten – Milgrom's sequential trading model allows only one trader to trade at a certain point in time, and only one unit can be delivered. Traders can decide whether to trade. After each transaction is over, the market maker uses Bayesian update to adjust the buying and selling price. If there is a sudden increase in buying orders in the securities market, the market maker will raise the selling price. This adjustment process is a Bayesian learning process.

(2) Easley – O's Hara sequential trading model. In this model, the number of transactions at a point in time is no longer a unit, but is divided into large transactions and small transactions. The uncertainties of information mainly include: Good news, bad news, and no news. Generally speaking, large orders are usually traded at a relatively low price. This model also analyzes the impact of transaction execution time on price, and finds that whether the transaction is completed will provide the market maker with certain information, that is to say, time also contains a certain amount of information, which will ultimately affect the size of the bid – ask spread.

2.2   Efficient market hypothesis

As early as 1900, Louis Bachelier developed that stock prices follow a random walk in the securities market. He first pointed out that stock prices follow a random walk in the speculative market; Subsequently, scholars such as Alfred Cowles (1933), Kendall (Maurice G. Kendall, 1953), and Kutner (Paul H. Cootner, 1964) successively conducted a large number of fruitful studies on this issue. Paul A. Samuelsen (1965) gave a more general mathematical explanation theoretically.

In 1965, Fama integrated various viewpoints and formally proposed the Efficient Market Hypothesis (EMH), stating: "An efficient market refers to a market where there are a large number of rational participants actively competing. In this market, everybody participants try their best to predict the market value of securities in the future, and the current important information is almost freely available to all participants. In an efficient market, the competition of participants leads to such a situation, at any point in time, the actual price of securities They have already reflected the information of events that have occurred and that the market expects events to occur in the future. That is to say, in an efficient market, the price of a security at any point in time is the best estimate of its intrinsic value. "

The efficient market hypothesis is the core of quantitative financial market theory and one of the important theoretical foundations of modern financial economics. At present, most of the classic financial theories we know are based on EMH theory, such as Markowitz's (1952) Modern Portfolio Theory (MPT), Sharp's (William F. Sharpe, 1964) Capital Asset Pricing Model (CAPM), and Black – Shules – Morton (Robert C. Merton, Fischer Black and Myron Scholes, 1973) option pricing model (OPM), Ross (Stephen A. Ross, 1976) arbitrage pricing model (APT), etc.

2. 2. 1 Assumptions

The assumptions of the efficient market theory mainly include: the securities market is frictionless; There are no transaction costs in the securities trading process; market participants do not need to pay additional costs to obtain information; investors are rational and also That is, the goal of investors is to maximize personal utility. Even if some investors are irrational, since their transactions in the market are mostly carried out randomly, when the number of such investors is large, their independent trading behaviors can offset each other to a large extent. Therefore, even if the trading volume of irrational investors is relatively large, the price of securities still changes near the basic value; on the other hand, because irrational investors usually buy high and sell low, this investment method will also lead to their wealth gradually. Decrease until it completely exits the securities market. Obviously, when investors are rational, security prices can "fully reflect" all available information in such a market. However, in the actual securities market, such a frictionless market is almost impossible to exist, but some supporters of the efficient market theory believe that these conditions are not necessary for the effectiveness of the securities market, and these conditions are appropriately relaxed to a certain extent. The stock market should still be effective.

2.2.2　Classification

In 1991, on the basis of Robert's (1967) information classification method, Fama divided the effective market into: weak effective market, semi – strong effective market, and strong effective market. The focus of efficient market theory is information. Generally speaking, information can be divided into historical information, publicly available information, and all available information. In 1967, Roberts proposed an information classification method. On this basis, Fama proposed three effective market forms in 1991 according to the availability of information and the cost of information acquisition:

(1) Weak – form Efficient Market Hypothesis. This hypothesis believes that the current price of financial assets has been fully reflected in all historical information, including past price trends, trading volumes, yields, etc. At this time, all historical information has been reflected in the security price, which means that it has nothing to do with future changes in security prices, so it is impossible to use historical information to predict the future, which means that the traditional reliance on the securities market. Technical analysis methods for indicators such as historical transaction prices and volume will lose their effectiveness.

(2) Semi – strong Form Efficient Market Hypothesis. The hypothesis believes that the security price not only reflects all the information in the historical price, but

also reflects all the public information, including: transaction price, trading volume, turnover rate, liquidity, price－earnings ratio, price－to－book ratio, corporate finance. Information, profit to the company, dividends, management characteristics, etc. Since the price of securities has already reflected all the publicly available information, investors cannot use publicly available information to obtain excess returns. Under the semi－strong efficient market hypothesis, any fundamental analysis in the securities market is also invalid, and it is impossible to rely on public information to obtain more accurate information than its competitors. At the same time, the information can be quickly reflected in the stock price once it is released, so any technical analysis and fundamental analysis will be invalid at this time, and only non－public information such as inside information can obtain excess returns.

(3) Strong－form Efficient Market Hypothesis. The hypothesis believes that the price of securities has reflected all information, including historical, published, and undisclosed information. At this time, no investor will be able to obtain excess returns in the securities market.

Under the strong efficient market hypothesis, the information related to the value of the company has been reflected in the price of the securities. At this time, all investors in the market have exactly all the information about the company, so no investor can obtain excess returns through information. It can be seen from the above expression that a strong efficient market is a very extreme situation. It requires securities prices to reflect the company's internal information, but the nature of internal information is non－publicity, so this situation is quite contradictory.

It can be seen from the above expression that the weak－form efficient market hypothesis reflects that the information set of securities prices is the smallest, only historical transaction information; while the information set of the semi－strong efficient market includes both the information set of the weak – form efficient market and

including all publicly available information; the strong effective market has the largest

information set, including not only the weak effective market and the semi – strong ef-

fective market, but also the information known to insiders. The information set be-

tween the three is from a small range to a large range, the latter includes the relation-

ship of the former, as shown in Figure 2. 1.

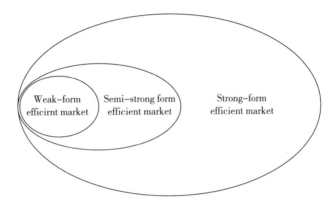

Figure 2. 1   Strong – Form, Semi – Strong, Weak – Form Efficient Market

If investors believe that the market is not efficient or in a weakly efficient state,

then investors should adopt an active investment strategy. The so – called active in-

vestment strategy means that investors actively collect information for analysis, try to

buy securities that are undervalued by the market, or sell securities that are overva-

lued by the market, so as to obtain excess returns. The most important part of adop-

ting an active investment strategy is stock selection and timing. Stock selection is the

selection of appropriate stocks; timing is the choice of a reasonable trading opportunity

by investors through estimation and judgment of factors such as the liquidity of the securities market.

In fact, it can be seen from the above analysis that if the securities market is strong and effective, then no matter what kind of investment strategy is used by any investor, it will not be able to obtain excess returns. Neither technical analysis nor basic analysis will be effective. However, even in a strong and efficient market, portfolio management strategies are effective. The reason is the principle of portfolio diversification. Through portfolio management strategies, investors can effectively reduce non – systematic risks in portfolio risks.

2. 2. 3　Testing the efficient market hypothesis

Since the emergence of the efficient market hypothesis, many academic scholars and industry experts have tested the effectiveness of the securities market through various empirical analyses. Most research results show that the stock market is weakly effective or semi – strongly effective. In fact, all the test results cannot completely reject the hypothesis that the market is efficient. This is because the empirical results reject the null hypothesis, either because the market is invalid or because the model is set incorrectly.

According to the classification of the effective market, we know that if the strong – form effective market hypothesis is established, then the semi – strong – form effective market hypothesis must also be established; and if the semi – strong – form effective market hypothesis is established, then the weak – form effective market hypothesis must also be established. Hence, when testing the securities market, the first step is to test whether the weak efficient market hypothesis is valid. If the weak efficient market hypothesis is valid, then continue to test whether the semi – strong efficient market hypothesis is valid; if the semi – strong efficient market hypothesis is valid it also holds, then check whether the strong efficient market hypothesis holds.

The test methods of the efficient market hypothesis theory mainly include:

(1) Serial Correlation. Serial correlation test is to test the autocorrelation of stock price changes, and test the correlation coefficient of stock price changes in period i and period j. If the correlation coefficient is high, then it means that the price change of the security is easily affected by the price change of the previous period; if the correlation coefficient is very low, then the change of the security price is serially uncorrelated, which means that investors cannot compare with the current price. Historical security price information is used to predict future security price changes, that is, the security market is weakly effective.

Correlation test is to test whether there is a linear relationship between the current rate of return of the security and the historical rate of return. The regression equation can be expressed as:

$$r_t = \alpha + \beta r_{t-k} + \varepsilon_t \tag{2.1}$$

Where, α represents the expected return which has nothing to do with historical yield; β indicates the correlation between the current rate of return and the historical rate of return; r_t and r_{t-k} respectively represent the rate of return of the period t and the period $t - k$; ε_t is the random interference items.

(2) Run tests. Run test, also known as continuous test, is a test method that judges the number of runs formed by the arrangement of sample performance. This is a non – parametric statistical hypothesis test method. It is the general term for the total number of runs test and the maximum run test. It is used to compare two independent samples and test the randomness of observation results. If the security rate of return is positive, then we will mark it as a " + " sign; otherwise, it will be marked as a " – " sign. A sequence with the same sign is called a run. Therefore, you can

use the analysis of the price change sequence. If the correlation is high, then a longer " + " sequence or " − " sequence will appear with a greater probability.

（3）Filter inspection. In 1964, Alexanda proposed the famous filtering test to verify whether the securities market reached a weak and effective. Subsequently, Fama and Blume（1966）extended the filtering principle. The so − called filter test means that if the stock price changes exceed the threshold set by the model, then it will continue to continue this change to a certain extent, which is the so − called momentum effect. Therefore, investors can select securities portfolios based on this information.

（4）The event study. Ball and Brown（1968）and Fama et al.（1969）proposed the event study. The principle of this method is relatively simple, intuitive and easy to use. The basic principle is to select a specific event according to the research purpose, and then analyze and explain the impact of the specific event on the sample stocks based on the changes in the return rate of the sample stocks before and after the research event. Obviously, according to Efficient Markets Hypothesis, if the securities market is a semi − strong efficient market, then any event will be immediately reflected in the security price, and no one can use this event to obtain excess returns. Therefore, the event research method is mainly used to test the semi − strong efficient market theory.

The basic steps of event study method are as follows:

1）Determine the research event according to the research purpose.

2）Determine the event period. The primary task of investigating the impact of events on securities prices is to establish a reasonable event period, which mainly includes the pre − estimation period and the post − event observation period. The main function of the pre − estimation period is to estimate the normal rate of return; the post – event observation period is mainly used to study the abnormal changes in securities prices after the event.

In summary, the advantages of the sequence correlation test method are simple and intuitive, easy to operate and implement; the disadvantage is that the results are easily affected by individual extreme values; the results of the run – length test are not easily affected by individual extreme values. Of course, both the serial correlation test and the run test reflect a correlation between the current rate of return and the previous rate of return.

2.3   Fractals theory

Modern Portfolio Theory (MTP) has been more than 60 years since its inception. The core issue of MTP research is how investors can diversify their risks and ensure returns by constructing investment portfolios to diversify their funds and invest in different assets. MTP is not only the beginning of modern finance, but also the driving force of modern financial theoretical research. It occupies an important position in financial theoretical research and financial practical operation. At present, a large number of scholars have conducted research on MTP and achieved some results. Although these results have enriched MTP, the existing results mainly use methods such as mean, variance, lower variance, fuzzy mathematics, conditional value at risk, and integrated forecast entropy to measure the returns and risks of securities when constructing investment portfolios. When securities prices have no fractal characteristics, methods such as mean, variance, downward bias, and fuzzy mathematics may be able to accurately measure the returns and risks of securities. However, a large number of studies have shown that securities prices generally have obvious fractal characteristics. For example, some scholars have empirically found that derivatives and spot markets have fractal characteristics, some scholars have empirically found that Shanghai and Shenzhen stock markets have multiple fractal characteristics, and some scholars have empirically found that the stock indexes of 32 countries all have fractal characteristics. At this time, using these methods to measure the returns and risks of securities has defects that are difficult or even impossible to measure accurately.

Specifically, when the security price has fractal characteristics, the fluctuation of the security price obeys the fractal Brownian motion, and the return rate of the securities obeys the fractal distribution, showing the characteristics of self – semilar, scale – invariance, and long – term memory, showing an infinitely fine complex structure. Scholars have clearly pointed out that fractal methods are a powerful tool to characterize securities whose prices have fractal characteristics; subsequent studies by a large number of scholars have shown that when the correct price has fractal characteristics, only the fractal method can be used to measure the return and return of securities. Risks and other characteristics, the results obtained may be accurate; it is difficult to accurately measure the return and risk characteristics of securities by using non – fractal methods such as mean, variance, lower variance, fuzzy mathematics. At the same time, according to the previous article, when the security price has fractal characteristics, the security return rate obeys the fractal distribution. Fractal distribution is a more complex power – law distribution, and its mean and variance may tend to be infinite; at this time, non – fractal methods such as mean, variance, and lower partial variance are used to measure the return and risk of securities, and it is impossible to measure the return and risk of securities. It can be seen that the existing research mainly uses non – fractal methods to measure the return and risk of securities, which has the flaws of uncertainty or unpredictability, which ultimately leads to the lack of effectiveness of the constructed investment portfolio.

In summary, the research on MTP has important theoretical and application value. The methods used by the existing related results to measure the return and risk of securities are mainly non – fractal methods. Under the realistic background that securities prices generally have fractal characteristics, there are uncertainties. Or unpredictable defects that affect the effectiveness of the investment portfolio.

Efficient market theory is the cornerstone of quantitative capital market theory and VaR risk measurement theory. As a linear research paradigm, it has dominated the theoretical research of quantitative investment finance for more than 40 years. Samuelson (1965) first proposed the efficient market theory, which showed that in an information – flowing market, if price changes can fully reflect the expectations and information possessed by all investors, the price is unpredictable. Fama (1970) made a great contribution to the formation and perfection of the efficient market theory. He proposed that in an efficient capital market, the movement process of asset prices can be described by martingale, according to the different degree of information reflected by asset prices. The market efficiency can be divided into three forms (see Figure 2.2): ①Weak – form efficiency: It is reflected in the historical information that the price completely reflects. In other words, an investor cannot understand the history of price changes. Information and use any technical methods to analyze their results to improve the ability to choose securities; ②Semi – strong efficiency: the price completely reflects the public information of the company under consideration, so the efforts to obtain and analyze this information cannot be expected to produce more Good results; ③Strongly effective: Even investors with privileged information (including insider) cannot often use it to guarantee excess investment returns.

| Weak efficiency | Semi–strong efficiency | Strong efficiency |

Figure 2. 2   Classification of Securities Market Effectiveness

However, the actual capital market is not completely effective and exhibits complex nonlinear fractal characteristics. Fractal[①] comes from the Latin fractus, which means "fragmented, split". Fractal Market Theory (Fractal Market Theory) is when Peters (1991, 1994) used R/S analysis to study the stock market, and applied the fractal thought created by Mandelbrot (1975) to the capital market. Put forward and analyze the shortcomings of the effective market theory in practice, break through the independent, linear, normal, random walk assumptions of the effective market theory, and emphasize the degree of market information reflection and the investment time scale from a non – linear perspective. It is believed that all stable markets have a fractal structure, which is a direct application of fractal geometry theory (see Table 2. 1 for the comparison of the properties of fractal geometry and Euclidean geometry) in the capital market. The theory believes that the capital market is composed of a large number of investors with different maturity structures. Information has different effects on the trading hours of various investors. The initial state will have a continuous and relevant relationship with future price changes, that is, assets. The price change is not a random walk, but a long memory with an enhanced trend. Frac-

---

① The term fractal was created by Mandelbrot, the father of fractal theory, in 1975, and published the book "Fractal: Opportunity, Form and Dimension" in French in the same year. In 1977, the book of the same name was translated into English and published in 1994 and 1996. Came to China twice a year to introduce fractal theory, and died in the United States on October 14, 2010.

tal market theory is a complex model based on a nonlinear dynamic mechanism, which appropriately relaxes the assumptions of efficient market theory. Therefore, its proposal makes the understanding of market and economic issues more complicated, and it is closer to the nonlinear nature of the capital market. Statistics feature. The difference and connection between the two are shown in Table 2. 1:

Table 2. 1　Comparison of properties between Euclidean geometry and fractal geometry

Indicator attributes	Euclidean geometry	Fractal geometry
Research object	Simple standard objects created by humans (continuous, differentiable, directable, regular, smooth)	Complex real objects created by nature (discontinuous, unguided, irregular, non – smooth)
Characteristic length	Yes	No
Hierarchical	No	Yes (Multifractal)
Similarity	No	Yes
Way of expression	Expressed by mathematical formulas	Express in iterative language, fractal dimension
Dimension	0 and positive integer	Generally a fraction, can be a positive integer
Dimensional Meaning	Describe the number of independent variables or degrees of freedom	Different fractal dimensions have different meanings

Table 2. 2　Differences and connections between efficient market theory and fractal market theory

Indicator attributes	Efficient market theory	Fractal market theory
Market characteristics	Linear, isolated system	Non – linear, open, dissipative system
Equilibrium	balanced	Allow disequilibrium
Complexity	Simple	Has the characteristics of fractal, chaos, etc.
Feedback mechanism	No	Positive feedback
Revenue sequence	White noise, independent	Fractional noise, long memory
Price series	Brownian motion ($H = 0.5$)	Fractional Brownian motion or biased random walk ($H \neq 0.5$)

Continued

Indicator attributes	Efficient market theory	Fractal market theory
Risk measurement method	Finite variance	Hurst Index and its promotion
Predictability	Not predictable	Provides a new method for forecasting
Volatility	Random	Presents a certain fractal law
Premise hypothesis	Investors are completely rational; Even if investors are not completely rational, random trading behaviors cancel each other out and will not affect asset price fluctuations; Even if investors are not completely rational and relevant, rational arbitrageurs will eliminate impact on asset prices	Investors are bounded and rational; Investors of different maturities respond to information in different degrees; The stability of the market is maintained by the market liquidity provided by investors of different maturities; Short – term market trends and There is no inherent consistency between long – term economic trends; In the short term, the capital market has a fractal statistical structure based on the long – term economic cycle
The connection between the two	The efficient market is a special case of the fractal market under linear conditions, and the normal distribution is a special case of the fractal distribution. The fractal market relaxes the assumption of the efficient market, making it closer to the realistic nonlinear market and accurately portraying it	

In fractal market theory, according to the particularity of the research object and the different research perspectives, fractals can be classified according to the following four attributes, as shown in Table 2. 3:

Table 2. 3　Different classifications of fractals

Classification attributes	Fractal name	Concept and meaning
Similarity	Strictly fractal	Strictly self – similarity between the part and the whole
	Statistical fractal	The part and the whole are only in a specific scale – free space, or self – similar at the statistical level

Continued

Classification attributes	Fractal name	Concept and meaning
Research object	Space fractal	Research objects are space objects such as coastlines, mountains and trees
	Time fractal	The research object is time series data such as stock prices
Similarity	Self – similar fractal	In a certain scale space, the fractal structure of any part of the local and the whole is consistent
	Self – affine fractal	If the scaling ratios of similar maps in all directions are not exactly the same, they have local self – affine properties
Complexity	Single fractal	The entire fractal body only needs one scale, one fractal dimension
	Multifractal	The entire fractal body needs multiple scales, multiple fractal dimensions

With the further in – depth study of the fractal characteristics of the capital market, it also raises some questions worth pondering: Can a fractal dimension better describe the entire fractal structure of the capital market? Is the long memory of the asset return sequence and its distribution on the time scale consistent? To answer these questions completely, a more detailed analysis of the local characteristics of the market fractal structure is necessary. If the fractal structure is uniform in each part, one fractal dimension can better describe its overall irregularity; if the fractal structure is non – uniform, it is difficult to describe its macroscopic structure with only one fractal dimension in general, local subsequences cannot be finely cut, and there is a lack of in – depth analysis of local singularities, that is, the non – linear complexity of asset price fluctuations cannot be fully described. In this regard, it is necessary to introduce multifractal theory to analyze the local features in more detail. This article combines fractal theory and advanced measurement models to test the long memory of the style asset index, empirically demonstrates the existence of a fractal structure in my country's fund market, and provides a realistic basis for fund managers to construct moderate style drift investment strategies to obtain short – term excess returns.

2. 4　Method system

2. 4. 1　Multi – fractal detrended fluctuation analysis (MF – DFA)

The common method to study multifractality in time series is multifractal detrended fluctuation analysis (MF – DFA), which uses different time scales to analyze the multifractal features of time series. This method can quantify the long – range correlation of time series and avoid artificially induced time series. MF – DFA method can not only judge whether liquidity has fractal characteristics, but also analyze the degree and the causes of multifractality. MF – DFA method can be described as follows.

Let us suppose that $\{x_i\}_{i=1}^N$ is a time series of length N.

Step 1: Calculate the mean $\bar{x}$ of the time series $\{x_i\}_{i=1}^N$ and use $X_b = \sum_{i=1}^b (x_i - \bar{x})$ to construct the cumulative deviation sequences $\{X_b\}_{b=1}^N$.

Step 2: Divide the sequences $\{X_b\}_{b=1}^N$ into $N_s \equiv \text{int}\left(\dfrac{N}{s}\right)$ non – lapping segments of equal length s, s represents the time scale, which is the length of the sub – window selected when observing the time series. If N divided by s is not an integer, a short part at the tail or the head of the sequences may be ignored. This paper assumes dividing the sequences from the tail of the series and defines the m th segment as $\{X_b^m\}$, $m = 1, 2, \cdots, N_s$, $b = (m-1)s + 1 + N - sN_s, \cdots, ms + N - sN_s$.

Step 3: Calculate the local trend for each of the N_s segments by a least – square fit of the sequences and get a local trend function $\overline{X}_k^m$. This trend function could be a linear, quadratic, cubic, or higher – order polynomial. When this polynomial is the l th order, the trends of order $l-1$ in original time series are eliminated. Calculate from the high order to the low order.

Step 4: Give the local variance of the time series:

$$F_m(s) = \frac{1}{s} \sum_{k=(m-1)s+1+N-sN_s}^{ms+N-sN_s} [X_k^m - \overline{X}_k^m]^2 \tag{2.2}$$

To ensure that the above formula is not zero and a high stability of $F_m(s)$, $F_m(s)$ is only defined for $\text{int}(0.25n) \geqslant s \geqslant l+2$.

Step 5: For N_s intervals average over all segments to obtain the qth order fluctuation function $F_q(s)$:

$$\begin{cases} F_q(s) = \left[\dfrac{1}{N_s}\sum_{m=1}^{N_s} F_m(s)^{\frac{q}{2}}\right]^{\frac{1}{q}}, & q \neq 0 \\[4mm] F_q(s) = \exp\left[\dfrac{1}{2N_s}\sum_{m=1}^{N_s} \ln F_m(s)\right], & q = 0 \end{cases} \tag{2.3}$$

when the absolute value of q is greater than a certain value, $F_q(s)$ will tend to be stable.

Step 6: For the fractal signals, if the series is long – range power – law correlated, $F_q(s)$ increases for large values of s, as a power – law.

$$F_q(s) \sim s^{h(q)} \tag{2.4}$$

In general, $h(q)$ may depend on q. If $h(q)$ is a constant which is independent on q, then the series is mono – fractal, or it is multifractal. When $q = 2$, $h(2)$ is the well – known Hurst exponent obtained by R/S analysis. If $h(2) = 0.5$, the original time series is an independent process following random walk process. If $0.5 <$

$h(2) \leqslant 1$, the correlations in the time series are persistence and long – range memory. If $0 \leqslant h(2) < 0.5$, the correlations in the time series are anti – persistence. We also employ the measure, $\Delta h = h(q_{min}) - h(q_{max})$ and $\Delta h \geqslant 0$, to quantify the degree of multifractality through the size of Δh . The larger Δh , the more severe the data fluctuates and the worse the efficiency of the market is.

Step 7: Identification of the trended fluctuations. The fluctuations of liquidity contain four phases: continuous upward stage, continuous downward stage, high reversal stage, and low reversal stage. At continuous upward or continuous downward stage, the liquidity that has risen or fallen in the earlier period continued to rise or fall in the later period. At high reversal or low reversal stage, the liquidity went up or down in the previous stage had a reversal change, the liquidity that went up or down started going down or up in the later stage.

2.4.2 Trendency entropy dimension model

If the market liquidity has fractal features, it is difficult to describe the nonlinear features of fractal time sequences by using a simple auto – correlation analysis method. Therefore, according to the description of the fractal theory by Falconer (2003), the entropy dimension D can effectively describe the consistency and reverse of the time sequence trend. When $1 < D < 1.5$, the sequence has the consistency of trend, corresponding to the continuous upward stage and continuous downward stage; when $1.5 < D < 2$, the sequence has reversion of trend, corresponding to high reversal stage and low reversal stage.

The entropy dimension D can effectively describe the trend of fractal sequences, but it can't distinguish whether the sequences are rising or falling. Therefore, we improve the entropy dimension D and increase its ability to identify the trend direction based on relevant papers, and the improved entropy dimensions are called rising or falling entropy dimensions and represented by D^+ and D^- respectively, they are collectively referred to the tendency entropy dimension.

In general, we support that $\{x_i\}_{i=1}^N$ is a series of length N, and calculate the length of time sequences curve according to the formula:

$$L(Y) = \sum_{i=1}^N |x_{i+1} - x_i| \tag{2.5}$$

Magnify the measuring scale R – fold, $R \in \{2^{-1} \times N, \cdots, 2^{-\mathrm{int}(\log_2 N)} \times N\}$. For the entropy dimension of different trends, when we construct the rising tendency entropy dimension D^+, the interval belonging to the downward trend is excluded from the time series, only the interval sequence of the rising trend is calculated, and the sequence curve length of the rising trend range under the formula (2.4) and formula (2.5) is calculated.

$$L^+(Y_R) = R^{-1} \sum_{i=1}^{R^{-1}N} M_i^+ \tag{2.6}$$

$$M_t^+ = \begin{cases} \max\limits_{R_i \leqslant t \leqslant R_i + R} \{x_t\} - \min\limits_{R_i \leqslant t \leqslant R_i + R} \{x_t\}, & x_{R_i+R} > x_{R_i} \\ 0, & x_{R_i+R} \leqslant x_{R_i} \end{cases} \tag{2.7}$$

Conversely, when we construct the falling entropy dimension D^-, only calculate the interval of the falling trend, and eliminate the rising trend interval according to formula (2.8) and formula (2.9):

$$L^-(Y_R) = R^{-1} \sum_{i=1}^{R^{-1}N} M_i^- \tag{2.8}$$

$$M_t^- = \begin{cases} \max\limits_{R_i \leqslant t \leqslant R_i + R} \{x_t\} - \min\limits_{R_i \leqslant t \leqslant R_i + R} \{x_t\}, & x_{R_i+R} < x_{R_i} \\ 0, & x_{R_i+R} \geqslant x_{R_i} \end{cases} \tag{2.9}$$

Finally, change the value of R, calculate $L^+(Y_R)$ or $L^-(Y_R)$, construct the double logarithmic coordinate $\ln R$ and $\ln L^+ (Y_R)$ or $\ln L^- (Y_R)$ and calculate the slope of the fitting line, the opposite of the slope is the rising or falling entropy dimension of the time series. Specifically, the calculation results of identifying continuous upward or downward stage and the high or low reversal stage can be divided into five situations:

Case 1: when $D^- \leqslant D$ and $D^- < 1.5$, or $1.5 > D^+ \geqslant D$, it is the continuous downward stage;

Case 2: when $D^+ \leqslant D$ and $D^+ < 1.5$, or $1.5 > D^- \geqslant D$, it is the continuous upward stage;

Case 3: when $D^+ \geqslant D$ and $D^+ > 1.5$, or $1.5 < D^- \leqslant D$, it is the low reversal stage;

Case 4: when $D^- \geqslant D$ and $D^- > 1.5$, or $1.5 < D^+ \leqslant D$, it is the high reversal stage;

Case 5: when $D^+ = 0$ or $D^- = 0$, the sequence is monotonically increasing or decreasing, then it is the continuous upward or downward stage.

Chapter 3   Liquidity Measurement and Its Influencing Factors in China's Financial Market

3.1   Liquidity measurement

Liquidity is one of the most important indicators reflecting the quality of financial markets. The quality of liquidity will directly affect the change of securities prices. If the stock market has perfect liquidity, the order of investors can be traded quickly and cheaply. When constructing investment strategy, investors should not only consider the stock price, but also consider whether the stock liquidity is enough. If liquidity is poor, then investors must bear additional transaction costs, namely liquidity costs, or market shock costs.

As one of the most important parts of investors' transaction costs, liquidity costs will directly affect the expected investment income. To complete the buy orders, the investor will bear the additional cost, namely the market shock; As the seller's investors, to complete the order transaction in time, will also lose part of the income. Market shocks cause investors to pay extra transaction costs, so investors always hate market shocks. To some extent, market shock is a transaction cost paid by investors to obtain additional market liquidity so that they can complete orders in a timely manner. However, for the whole securities market, the market shock has obviously two sides. On the one hand, market shock will increase the degree of stock price fluctuation at some time, increasing the market volatility; On the other hand, in some cases, market shocks can, to some extent, slow down the change of stock prices, reduce the volatility of the market and improve the stability of the market.

To measure the scale of market shocks, many scholars propose using one indicator to depict the market price at which investors have no particular order, such as yesterday's closing price (Kogan, 2006), average of the highest and lowest prices of the securities on the trading Days (Blum et al., 1986), average of the highest, lowest, opening and closing prices of the securities on the trading Days (Domowitz et al., 2001), Volume Weighted Average Price (VWAP) (Berkowitz and Logue, 1988), etc. Since the market shock is the influence of investors' orders on security prices, many scholars estimate the market shock from the volume – price relationships, namely using the regression coefficient between the trading volume and changes in security price, which is also known as the market shock coefficient (Kyle, 1985; Glosten and Harris, 1988). On this basis, Lillo et al. (2003) proposed a market shock function, pointing out that the scale of market shocks is closely related to the trading volume and market liquidity. Chen et al. (2010) analyzed the influence of the orders difference, the trading volume change and other factors on market shocks, and pointed out that there is a positive correlation between the orders diffe-rence, market trading volume change and security price change. Further, Alzahrani et al. (2013) and Ryu (2013) respectively studied the possible factors of market shocks for Saudi security market and Korean futures market, and pointed out that there is a significant positive correlation between the size of investors' orders and market shocks. In order to clarify the relationship between the trading volume and market shocks, Huberman, Stanzl (2004) and Almgren et al. (2005) theoretically proved that permanent market shocks have a linear relationship with trading volume, while for temporary market shocks, the relationship with trading volume maybe either linear or nonlinear.

Generally speaking, for the large – cap stock of particularly large circulating market value, its liquidity is generally better so that the market shock is relatively less in the process of trading. However, in China's security market, some large – cap stocks have a very large circulating market value, their liquidity may not be as good as their circulation market value. As can be shown in Table 3. 1, the circulation mar-ket value of ICBC (601398), a large – cap stock, is about one trillion, while that of Letv (300104), a GEM stock, is only billions. Nevertheless, from the perspective of turnover rate, the liquidity of Letv is much better than that of ICBC. Therefore, from the perspective of liquidity, based on the index of turnover rate and model of Kyle (1985) and Chiyachantana et al. (2004), this study describes the scale of market shocks by using the regression coefficient of stock trading volume and price change, and analyzes the factors of security market shocks by using the high – frequency trading data in China's security market.

Table 3.1 Comparison of typical large – cap and small – cap indicators

Stock code	Name	Shareholding ratio of top ten shareholders（%）	Annual trading amount（10 billion）	Annual circulation market value of shares（10 billion）	Annual turnover rate
601398	ICBC	97.03	42.62	1,090.72	3.95
300104	Letv	10.39	45.71	3.05	1,191.24

3.1.1   Internal mechanism of liquidity cost

Liquidity cost is an important transaction cost in the transaction process of investors. It is particularly important to study and estimate the scale of liquidity. Suppose the market price of the stock at the time t_0 is p_0, and at the time t_1 is p'_1, then during the period $[t_0, t_1]$ the change of the stock price is $\Delta p = p'_1 - p_0$. If the investor submits a purchase order（B）to the market for trading at the time t_0, and the stock price is p_1 at the time t_1, in this case, during the period $[t_0, t_1]$ the change of the stock price is $\Delta p' = p'_1 - p_0$. Clearly, investors in the real stock market can't observe both of the above stock price changes at the same time, and investors pay more attention to the impact of their submitted orders on the stock price, therefore, the stock price changes mentioned in the following paragraphs particularly refer to "the stock price movements when investors order in the market".

According to the definition of the market shock, the market shock（*MI*）on order（B）is：

$$MI = p_1 - p'_1 \tag{3.1}$$

According to the above equation, the relationship between the market shock, stock price changes and stock price changes when this order B does not exist in the market is as follows:

$$MI = p_1 - p'_1$$

$$= (p_1 - p_0) - (p'_1 - p_0)$$

$$= \Delta p - \Delta p' \tag{3.2}$$

Transferring Equation (3.2), we can get:

$$\Delta p = \Delta p' + MI \tag{3.3}$$

It can be seen from Equation (3.3) that the relationship between the market shock and stock price changes is as follows:

(1) If the stock price in the market (the stock price without order B) is in a period of rise, namely $\Delta p' > 0$, the market shock will make the stock price changes more sharply.

(2) If the stock price in the market (the stock price without order B) is in a period of decline, namely $\Delta p' < 0$, now the market shock will make the stock price changes tend to moderate.

(3) If the stock price in the market (the stock price in the absence of order B) is in a stable period, namely $\Delta p' = 0$, now all the changes in stock prices come from the market shock.

If at the time t_0 the investor submits a sell order (S) to the market for trading, and at the time t_1 the stock price is p_1, in this case, during the period $[t_0, t_1]$ the price change of the stock is $\Delta p' = p'_1 - p_0$.

According to the definition of market shock, the market shock on the sell order (S) is:

$$MI = - (p_1 - p'_1) \tag{3.4}$$

According to the above equation, the relationship between the market shock, stock price changes and stock price changes when this order B does not exist in the market is as follows:

$$MI = -(p_1 - p'_1)$$

$$= (p'_1 - p_0) - (p_1 - p_0)$$

$$= \Delta p' - \Delta p \qquad\qquad (3.5)$$

Transferring Equation (3.5), we can get:

$$\Delta p = \Delta p' - MI \qquad\qquad (3.6)$$

It can be seen from Equation (3.6), the relationship between the above market shock and stock price changes is as follows:

(1) If the stock price in the market (the stock price without selling order S) is in a period of rise, namely $\Delta p' > 0$, the market shock will slow down the stock price changes.

(2) If the stock price in the market (the stock price without selling order S) is in a period of decline, namely $\Delta p' < 0$, now the market shock increases the stock price changes.

(3) If the stock price in the market (the stock price without selling order S) is in a stable period, namely $\Delta p' = 0$, now the changes of the stock price are consistent with the changes of the market shock.

3.1.2 Measurement of liquidity

Suppose the investor submits the orders to the market in period 0 and will execute orders within next n trading periods. In random trading period t, the change of a security price is Δp_t, and the volume of trading is v_t. Kyle (1985) analyzed the impact of investors' net trading behavior (the difference between the buyer's demand and the seller's demand in the same period) on the changes of security price, and its model can be expressed as follows:

$$\Delta p_t = \lambda v_t \tag{3.7}$$

Thereinto, λ represents the extent to which the expected market trading volume affects the changes of security price.

During the whole trading period, the relationship between the total trading volume of security and changes of price is as follows:

$$\sum_{t=1}^{n} \Delta p_t = \lambda \sum_{t=1}^{n} v_t \tag{3.8}$$

Divide Equation (3.7) by Equation (3.8) to get:

$$\frac{\Delta p_t}{\Delta P} = \frac{v_t}{V} \tag{3.9}$$

Thereinto, ΔP is the amount of the price change during the whole trading period; V represents the total volume of transactions during the whole trading period.

After all the orders are executed, the expected price of the security is:

$$
\begin{aligned}
E(p) &= \sum_{t=1}^{n} p_t \Pr(p = p_t) \\
&= \sum_{t=1}^{n} p_t \frac{\Delta p_t}{\Delta P} \\
&= \sum_{t=1}^{n} p_t \frac{v_t}{V}
\end{aligned}
\tag{3.10}
$$

Thereinto, $\Pr(p = p_t)$ is at time t the probability that the security price is p_t.

According to the expression form $P_{VWAP} = \sum_{t=1}^{n} \frac{p_t v_t}{V}$ of VWAP, the expected future price of security actually is the trading volumn – weighted average price in a trading period, namely VWAP.

This paper uses VWAP benchmark price to calculate price shock cost, namely price shock cost is equal to the difference between orders execution price and VWAP benchmark price. Since prices of different securities may vary greatly, the method of

Hu (2009) and Chiyachantana et al. (2004) is used for standardization of price shocks, namely:

$$PI_i = \frac{Side_i \times (P_i - vwap_i)}{P_i} \tag{3.11}$$

Thereinto, PI_i is the price shock cost of No. i transaction, P_i is the transaction price of No. i transaction; $Side_i$ is an identifying variable, if No. i transaction is initiated by the buyer, then $Side_i = 1$, if initiated by the seller, then $Side_i = -1$; $vwap_i$ is the trading volume weighted average price corresponding to No. i transaction.

3.2   Influencing factors

3.2.1   Hypotheses

Generally speaking, investors who hold the same amount of funds will be hit less by market shocks in large – cap stocks than in small – cap stocks. In China's security market, there are some securities with hundreds of billions or even trillions in circulation market value, their liquidity is not as good as its circulation market value. As can be seen from Table 1, the circulation market value of ICBC (601398), a large – cap stock, is 1.09 trillion, and its liquidity index—annual turnover rate is 3.95; The circulation market value of Letv (300104) on the GEM is only 305 million, while its annual turnover rate is 1,191.24. It can be seen from these indicators that although the circulation market value of ICBC is much higher than LeTV, its liquidity is far behind LeTV. The root cause of this phenomenon is the ownership structure. The top

10 ICBC's shareholders hold 97. 03% of the circulation shares, while the top 10 LeTV's shareholders hold only 10. 39%. Therefore, it is impossible to judge the scale of market shocks according to the size of the circulation market value. Based on this, this paper proposes the following hypotheses:

H1: For investors in the security market, the circulation market value is not the main factor affecting their liquidity.

Liquidity is the ability of orders to be traded quickly without causing dramatic changes in security prices (Hasbrouck and Schwartz, 1988; Loderer et al. , 1991; Doyne et al. , 2004; Liu Ti, 2012). Under the assumption of traditional investment theory, the stock market has perfect liquidity, which also means that investors' orders can be traded quickly and at low cost. In fact, in the process of orders trading, investors may be affected by the limited liquidity in the real security market, and at this time investors may bear larger market shocks. Therefore, liquidity is an important factor affecting market shocks, and turnover rate is an important indicator to measure the liquidity of the security market (Domowitz et al. , 2001; Zhang Yulong and Li Yizong, 2013; Liu Xiangli and Chang Yunbo, 2015). Therefore, this paper proposes the following hypotheses:

H2: For investors in the security market, turnover rate is an important factor affecting liquidity.

3. 2. 2   Sample selection

This study mainly considers the impact of circulation market value and liquidity on market shocks, using the high – frequency trading data provided by Shanghai Wind Information Technology Co. , Ltd. , the time span of the data is 4 January 2013 – 31 December 2013 – 20 stock samples were selected according to the size of stock circulation market value, including 10 large – cap stocks and 10 small – cap stocks. Delete data with obvious recording errors, as well as data with missing corresponding indicators.

3. 2. 3 Related variables

The explained variable in this study is the market shock, the main explaining variable is the circulation market value and turnover rate of individual stocks, and the control variable is the index of orders size and market turnover rate. The scale of market shocks is equal to the difference between the stock price after the execution of a particular order and the stock price when the order does not exist in the security market.

In fact, in the real security market, investors cannot observe these two prices at the same time. In order to estimate the scale of market shocks, this paper uses the model of Kyle (1985) and Chiyachantana et al. (2004) to describe the scale of market shocks by using the regression coefficient of stock price change and trading volume, namely:

$$\Delta p_t = \lambda_0 + \lambda_1 volume_t + \varepsilon_t \qquad (3.12)$$

Thereinto, λ_1 represents the market impact factor of the stock, Δp_t is the change of the stock price from period $t - 1$ to period t, namely: $\Delta p_t = p_t - p_{t-1}$; $volume_t$ represents the volume of transactions during the period t, positive if the order is initiated by the buyer or negative if the order is initiated by the seller.

In the study of market shocks, the order size of investors is an important indicator. Since the account trading data of specific investors cannot be obtained from the relevant trading data in China's security market, this study mainly uses the expected external trading volume in the market to represent the total order size of investors

(*size*), that is the difference between the trading volume and the average trading volume in the past period (5 Days in this study) . Meanwhile, the order size has been standardized.

For the security market, liquidity is an important factor reflecting its quality. Liquidity will have a direct impact on the speed at which investors execute their orders and the scale of market shocks. The moderate increase of liquidity can not only ensure the normal operation of the financial market, but also improve the allocation of resources in the security market. Liquidity is closely related to the range of security price changes. If the security market has good liquidity, then investors' orders can be executed in a period of time at low cost; On the contrary, if the security market lacks sufficient liquidity, investors will bear larger market shock cost in the transaction process. This study uses common turnover rate (*turnoverrate*) index to describe stock liquidity.

3. 2. 4   Descriptive statistics

The sample selected in this study consists of 20 stocks, including 10 large – cap stocks with larger circulation market value and 10 small – cap stocks. The time span of the sample is 4 January 2013 – 31 December 2013. Table 3. 2 is the selected stock samples' indexes of trading amount, circulation market value and turnover rate in 2013. As can be seen from Table 3. 2, the average circulation market value of large – cap stocks is about 432. 21 billion yuan, much higher than that of small – cap stocks (1. 2 billion yuan) . However, from the perspective of turnover rate, the liquidities of large – cap stocks selected in this study are poorer, with an average value of only 58. 83, far lower than that of small – cap stocks of 1, 313. 53, and also lower than the average turnover rate of all stocks in the secuity market of 469. 03 in 2013.

Table 3. 2   Amount of securities traded and market value in circulation in 2013

Stock code	Annual transaction amount (10 billion)	Annual circulation market value (10 billion)	Annual turnover rate
600028	48. 56	484. 68	10. 11
600031	87. 19	74. 46	103. 70
600036	134. 91	242. 91	66. 80
600048	112. 71	97. 08	150. 55
601088	72. 07	413. 48	17. 84
601166	154. 51	180. 03	106. 49
601328	55. 22	161. 58	36. 64
601398	42. 62	1, 090. 72	3. 95
601668	52. 79	117. 00	95. 37
601857	33. 08	1, 460. 16	2. 17
300051	18. 75	1. 05	2, 002. 72
300055	15. 96	1. 98	1, 592. 44
300077	7. 73	0. 62	625. 18
300084	45. 71	3. 05	1, 986. 77
300085	17. 69	0. 93	938. 01
300104	16. 02	1. 14	1, 191. 24
300118	10. 69	1. 07	637. 49
300155	3. 36	0. 30	1, 599. 80
300157	11. 05	0. 63	636. 08
300162	12. 19	1. 23	1, 925. 58

Table 3. 3 is the correlation matrix between selected stock samples and SSE Composite Index, Industrial and Commercial Bank of China (601398) and other stocks. As can be seen from Table 3. 3, compared with large – cap stocks, small – cap stocks have less correlation with the SSE Composite Index, and Industrial and Commercial Bank of China has a higher correlation with other stocks. Much recent volatility of stock prices started in large – cap stocks, followed by rapid changes in

other stocks and market indexes.

Table 3. 3   Correlation matrix between stock and market

	300051	300055	300077	300084	300085	300104	300118	300155	300157	300162
Market index	0. 09	0. 06	0. 12	0. 15	0. 28	0. 06	0. 08	0. 16	0. 17	0. 01
601398	0. 08	0. 08	0. 24	0. 11	0. 08	0. 05	0. 18	0. 09	0. 08	0. 21
	600028	600031	600036	600048	601088	601166	601328	601398	601668	601857
Market index	0. 18	0. 17	0. 26	0. 19	0. 34	0. 09	0. 21	0. 18	0. 36	0. 23
601398	0. 02	0. 20	0. 14	0. 07	0. 11	0. 10	0. 26	1. 00	0. 15	0. 01

This study uses 30 minutes as a trading period, the whole trading Days can be divided into eight different trading periods, namely the first trading period is 09: 30 – 10: 00, the second trading period is 10: 01 – 10: 30, the third trading period is 10: 31 – 11: 00, the fourth trading period is 11: 01 – 11: 30, the fifth trading period is 13: 01 – 13: 30, the sixth trading period is 13: 31 – 14: 00, the seventh trading period is 14: 01 – 14: 30, the last trading period is 14: 31 – 15: 00. According to (Hengyu Liu, 2008; Xingqiang He and Hong Niu, 2009; Xiangli Liu and Shouyang Wang, 2013) the relevant research shows that in the whole trading day, the liquidity in the stock market is better at the opening and closing. Therefore, in addition to taking the whole trading day as the research object, the first and last trading periods of every day are also selected for research.

Table 3.4, Table 3.5 and Table 3.6 respectively describe the descriptive statistical results of market shock factor (λ), individual stock turnover rate (*turnoverrate*), circulation market value (*dsmvosd*), order size (*size*), average market turnover rate (*markettor*) and other indicators during the whole trading day, the first trading period and the last trading period of each trading day. Table 3.7 shows the correlation coefficient matrix among variables in the whole trading day.

Table 3.4   Descriptive statistics (The whole trading day)

Variable	Mean value	Median	Max	Min	Standard deviation
λ	7. 84E – 07	4. 13E – 07	3. 58E – 05	9. 00E – 10	2. 16E – 06
turnoverrate	2. 76	0. 87	38. 53	0. 0022	4. 39
dsmvosd	2. 10E + 11	4. 40E + 10	1. 71E + 12	2. 49E + 08	3. 90E + 11
size	0. 0026	0. 0079	0. 3529	0. 0005	0. 0381
markettor	0. 74	0. 71	1. 71	0. 39	0. 2155

Table 3.5   Descriptive statistics (The first trading period)

Variable	Mean value	Median	Max	Min	Standard deviation
λ	6. 26E – 07	3. 01E – 07	1. 91E – 05	2. 00E – 9	7. 92E – 07
turnoverrate	2. 76	0. 87	38. 53	0. 0022	4. 39
dsmvosd	2. 10E + 11	4. 40E + 10	1. 71E + 12	2. 49E + 08	3. 90E + 11
size	0. 0174	0. 0091	0. 3529	0. 0019	0. 0117
markettor	0. 74	0. 71	1. 71	0. 39	0. 2155

Table 3.6   Descriptive statistics (The last trading period)

Variable	Mean value	Median	Max	Min	Standard deviation
λ	7. 14E – 07	3. 13E – 07	1. 58E – 05	9. 00E – 10	9. 16E – 07
turnoverrate	2. 76	0. 87	38. 53	0. 0022	4. 39
dsmvosd	2. 10E + 11	4. 40E + 10	1. 71E + 12	2. 49E + 08	3. 90E + 11
size	0. 0070	0. 0055	0. 1182	0. 0013	0. 0054
markettor	0. 74	0. 71	1. 71	0. 39	0. 2155

Table 3.7   Variable correlation coefficients (The whole trading day)

Variable	λ	dsmvosd	turnoverrate	markettor	size
λ	1. 0000 —				
dsmvosd	– 0. 1411 (0. 0000)	1. 0000 —			

Continued

Variable	λ	dsmvosd	turnoverrate	markettor	size
turnoverrate	−0. 2378	−0. 2188	1. 0000		
	(0. 0000)	(0. 0000)	—		
markettor	−0. 0063	0. 0194	0. 1205	1. 0000	
	(0. 4397)	(0. 0176)	(0. 0000)	—	
size	0. 2239	0. 1262	0. 1823	0. 2316	1. 0000
	(0. 0000)	(0. 0000)	(0. 0000)	(0. 0000)	—

3. 2. 5　Regression analysis and results

In this study, the market shock is the explained variable, the circulation market value and turnover rate of individual stocks are the explaining variables, and the order size and the average market turnover rate are the control variables. This study firstly regards each trading day as a trading period, uses the cross – section fixed effect model in panel data analysis to conduct regression estimation, and standardizes the circulation market value in the regression analysis. The results are shown in Table 3. 8.

Table 3. 8　Market shock regression results (The whole trading day)

Variable	Model 1	Model 2	Model 3	Model 4	Model 5
turnoverrate	−0. 0002 ***				−0. 0002 ***
	(0. 0000)				(0. 0000)
dsmvosd		−0. 0013		−0. 00001	
		(0. 2160)		(0. 9919)	
size			0. 0995 ***	0. 0995 ***	0. 0564 ***
			(0. 0000)	(0. 0000)	(0. 0020)
markettor			−0. 0015 ***	−0. 0015 ***	−0. 0010 ***
			(0. 0001)	(0. 0002)	(0. 0088)
AdjR^2	0. 65	0. 64	0. 64	0. 64	0. 65

Note: The values in brackets are the values corresponding to the estimated coefficients. ***, **, * indicate significant at 1%, 5% and 10% confidence level respectively. The same below.

It can be seen from Model 1 and Model 2 in Table 3.8, the turnover rate has a significant negative impact on market shocks, while the circulation market value has no significant impact on market shocks. It can be seen from Model 3 that the order size and market average turnover rate as control variables have a significant impact on the market shock. It can be seen from Model 4 that after controlling the order size and average market turnover rate, the circulation market value still has no significant impact on the market shock, namely, hypothesis 1 is true. The reason for this phenomenon may be that many large - cap stocks have a very large circulation market value, but a large part of their circulation stocks have been in a state of non - current for a long time, so their real liquidity is poorer. It can be seen from Model 5 that after controlling the order size of investors and the average market turnover rate, the turnover rate index of individual stocks has a significant negative impact on market shocks, namely, hypothesis 2 is true.

Next, for the first trading period and last trading period of each day, the market shock is the explained variable, the circulation market value and turnover rate of individual stocks are the explaining variables, the order size and market average turnover rate are the control variables, regression estimation use cross - section fixed effects model in panel data analysis, the results are shown in Table 3.9.

Table 3.9 Market shock regression results (The first trading period)

Variable	Model 6	Model 7	Model 8	Model 9	Model 10
turnoverrate	- 0.0002 *** (0.0000)				- 0.0003 *** (0.0000)
dsmvosd		- 0.0013 (0.2160)		- 0.0001 (0.7139)	

Continued

Variable	Model 6	Model 7	Model 8	Model 9	Model 10
size			0. 1273 ***	0. 1273 ***	0. 0847 ***
			(0. 0000)	(0. 0000)	(0. 0001)
markettor			−0. 0010 ***	−0. 0010 ***	−0. 0005 ***
			(0. 0000)	(0. 0001)	(0. 0008)
AdjR^2	0. 65	0. 64	0. 64	0. 64	0. 65

Table 3. 10   Market shock regression results (The eighth trading period)

Variable	Model 11	Model 12	Model 13	Model 14	Model 15
turnoverrate	−0. 0002 ***				−0. 0001 ***
	(0. 0000)				(0. 0000)
dsmvosd		−0. 0013		−0. 0001	
		(0. 2160)		(0. 8129)	
size			0. 1015 ***	0. 1015 ***	0. 0714 ***
			(0. 0000)	(0. 0000)	(0. 0012)
markettor			−0. 0011 ***	−0. 0011 ***	−0. 0008 ***
			(0. 0001)	(0. 0002)	(0. 0007)
AdjR^2	0. 65	0. 64	0. 64	0. 64	0. 65

In Table 3. 9 and Table 3. 10, it can be seen from Model 7 and Model 12 that the circulation market value has no significant impact on market shocks. It can be seen from Model 6 and Model 11 that the turnover rate index has a significant negative impact on market shocks. Even after controlling the order size and market turnover rate, it can be seen from Model 9, Model 10, Model 14 and Model 15 that the circulation market value has no significant impact on market shocks, while the turnover rate has a significant negative impact on market shocks. Namely, Hypothesis 1 and Hypothesis 2 are ture.

The above results show that if the stock has a good liquidity, then market shocks are less. For investors, investing in stocks with a higher turnover rate will result in less market shocks and higher potential investment return. From the perspective of supervision, regulators should focus on supervision of large stocks with lower turnover rate.

3. 3　Summary

In this study, the method of Kyle (1985) and Chiyachantana et al. (2004) is used to estimate market shocks of sample securities, theoretically analyze the relationship between market shocks and stock price changes, and study the impact of market shocks on stock price changes. At the same time, based on the historical high－frequency trading data of China's security market, the scale of market shocks is estimated, and the trading day is divided into eight different trading periods, and analyze the impact of the circulation market value, turnover rate and order size on market shocks.

The results show that although the market shock is an extra cost for investors, it has both disadvantages and advantages for the whole security market. For investors, if the stock price is in a rising stage and the order is executed at this time, market shocks will increase the price of the stock. If the stock price is in a declining stage and the order is executed at this time, market shocks will slow down the decline of the stock price, make the stock price changes tend to moderation, and reduce the volatility of the security market. The turnover rate is a significant factor affecting market shocks, while the circulation market value, which is more concerned by investors, has no significant impact on market shocks. For large – cap stocks with a smaller turnover rate, although the circulation market value is large, the total transaction amount is relatively smaller, so the market shock is greater, and the stock price is also vulnerable to the impact of large orders. Therefore, no matter for ordinary investors or institutional investors, they should pay much attention on stocks with a higher turnover rate in the investment process. For the regulators, they should focus on large – cap stocks with less liquidity in order to prevent the stock market price from dramatic fluctuations.

Chapter 4 Non – linear Characterization and Trend Identification of Liquidity in China's New OTC Stock Market

4. 1 Introduction

To promote the development of small and medium – sized technology – based enterprises and enhance these enterprises's financing efficiency, China established the new Over – the – Counter (OTC) stock market in 2006 and introduced the market – making system in 2014. The OTC stock market is an emerging market, compared with other markets, the liquidity of the new OTC market is still lacking and the liquidity risk is high. To improve the market liquidity in the new OTC market and reduce the market liquidity risk, it is of great theoretical and practical value to study market liquidity's features of the new OTC market.

Liquidity is not only an important factor of the price change in the stock, but also a significant index that reflects the quality of the stock market. High liquidity can promote the efficient operation of the stock market, the lack of liquidity will significantly affect the stable operation in the stock market. On August 16, 2013, the Everbright Securities only used more than 7 billion RMB to make more than 30 large – cap stocks closed to the upper limit in a few minutes, and the Shanghai Composite Index rose more than 5% in just one minute. China's stock market experienced a financial crisis in 2015, during this period, the new OTC stock market had been hit hard, the National Equities Exchange and Quotations (NEEQ) market – making component fell from the highest point 2,503. 06 on April 3 to 1,103. 78 on July 8. These events reveal that the severe lack of liquidity could cause instability in the stock market and also show that the liquidity is an important factor affecting the price volatility of securities. However, there is no consensus on the definition of liquidity in the academic community. Scholars can interpret the liquidity from four aspects: width, depth, timeliness, and elasticity. The width is the difference between the price signed by the effective price of the buyer and the seller in the market, and the main indicators: bid – ask spread, effective price difference, etc. The depth is the maximum trading volume that can be reached without affecting the current price, and the main indicators: Kyle depth indicator, Glostern – Harris indicator, transaction rate, and turnover rate, etc. The timeliness refers to the time required for a certain number of market exchanges, such as transaction frequency (Lippman and McCall), etc. The elasticity refers to the speed at which the exchange causes price fluctuations to disappear.

The change of the market is a stochastic process. Many studies have found that the change of the market is not strictly random, but long memory and self – similarity even in the most competitive market, the market has the characteristics of long memory and self – similarity. With the development of technology, the multifractal theory can obtain different fluctuation information of the market on different time scales and provide more analysis for the financial market. The multifractal theory is mainly used to study the rate of return and stock price index. For different time scales, Kantelhardt et al. propose the multifractal detrended fluctuation analysis (MF – DFA), this method can determine the multifractal scale of time series and distinguish the generalized probability density function and the multifractality of long – range correlation. Some authors use the MF – DFA to study the features of the stock market and find that the stock indexes have long – term correlation and multifractal features. For China's stock market, domestic scholars also find that China's stock market has long – term correlation and multifractal features.

Bernstein puts forward the concept of the momentum life cycle (MLC) and uses this method to analyze the mutual conversion relationship between momentum effect and the reversal effect of time series. Later, some authors prove the existence and performance features of MLC. Multifractal features of the stock market make it difficult to construct the identification measure of MLC. For the fractal market, Mandelbrot considers that it is more effective to study the stock market by using the fractal analysis method, Falconer uses the entropy dimension to effectively describe the trend fluctuation of the fractal time series, Yan and Wu use the "trend dimension" to effectively identify and measure the MLC of the fractal market. However, these analyses have not been performed on the fluctuation trend of market liquidity, so we use the "trend dimension" to study the fluctuation trend of market liquidity.

In summary, the market liquidity is so important and the volatility characteristic is the basis for liquidity's analysis, it is necessary to analyze liquidity's volatility characteristic. Under the background of fractal characteristics in the stock market, liquidity, as the core element of the stock market, is likely to have fractal characteristics. Hence it is difficult to investigate the possible fractal features by using non – fractal methods such as traditional financial models, and only fractal analysis methods can be accurately characterized and captured. Therefore, we choose the liquidity index of the new OTC market and use MF – DFA to study the multifractal features of liquidity. To analyze the multifractal degree of liquidity in the new OTC market, we use the Shanghai 50 index constituent stocks as the control group and compare the multifractal degree of liquidity between two markets. We also analyze the sources of multifractality and use the tendency entropy dimension to identify the trended fluctuations of liquidity. The study of liquidity characteristics can not only help investors reduce transaction costs and improve investment income, but also can provide a relevant reference for the relevant government departments to formulate regulatory policies, prevent the drastic volatility in the stock market and promote the healthy development of the stock market.

The remainder of the paper is organized as follows: Section 4. 2 mainly focuses on the description of the method. Section 4. 3 describes the data and index selection of market liquidity in the new OTC stock market. Section 4. 4 provides the empirical results, which include descriptive statistics of liquidity, multifractal analysis, sources of multifractality analysis, the identification of the trended fluctuations, and robustness test. Section 4. 5 is the conclusion.

4.2　Data description

A liquid market presents four different dimensions: width, depth, timeliness, and elasticity. China's new OTC market has been established for a short time, if we use the width index such as bid – ask spread to measure the market liquidity, the diversity of data selection is inadequate. To ensure that the index reflects the liquidity of China's new OTC market, we will select the depth index and use two methods to measure market liquidity.

Method 1: In the measurement of the liquidity, the turnover rate is one of the most common indicators, which is the ratio of volume to the number of shares in circulation, the calculation is as follow:

$$L_{i,t}^1 = Q_{i,t}/M_{i,t} \tag{4.1}$$

Where, $L_{i,t}^1$, $Q_{i,t}$ and $M_{i,t}$ represent the liquidity, the trading volume and the number of tradable shares respectively, i stands for the ith stock, t is the tth day.

Method 2: This index uses daytime price amplitude to replace the daily rate of return. Because of factors such as external market environment, the daily rate of return cannot accurately reflect the price impact caused by the investor's order.

While the daytime price amplitude can avoid some non – trading factors and eliminate the difference between the absolute price change and the tradable shares. The calculation is as follow:

$$L_{i,t}^2 = CHANGE_{i,t}/AMP_{i,t} \tag{4.2}$$

Where, $L_{i,t}^2$, $CHANGE_{i,t}$ and $AMP_{i,t}$ represent the liquidity, turnover rate, and daytime price amplitude respectively, i stands for the ith stock, t is the tth day.

This paper focuses on market liquidity, so we use the weighted average method to calculate the market liquidity by calculated as follows:

$$ML_t^1 = \sum_{i=1}^{n} (X_{i,t}L_{i,t}^1) \tag{4.3}$$

$$ML_t^2 = \sum_{i=1}^{n} (X_{i,t}L_{i,t}^2) \tag{4.4}$$

Where, $X_{i,t}$ is the ratio of a stock's current market value to the total sample stock's current market value, ML_t^1 and ML_t^2 are the market liquidity calculated by method 1 and 2, i stands for the i_{th} stock, t is the t_{th} day.

This paper uses the trading data in the new OTC market. The sample period is from January 1 to December 31 in 2018. We eliminate the stocks listed on the new OTC market after January 1 in 2018 and the stocks that have not been traded for the whole year of 2018. In this case, we have 990 stocks and 54,331 observations in total. Besides, to compare and analyze the multifractal degree of liquidity in the new OTC market and the large – cap market, we use SSE 50 constituent stock as the control group and eliminate the stocks listed after January 1, 2018 (601138. SH and 603259. SH are listed after January 1, 2018). All data comes from CSMAR, RES-SET, and the company's annual report.

4.3   Empirical research

4.3.1   Descriptive statistics of liquidity

To test whether the liquidity in the new OTC market is non – linear or not, we provide a descriptive statistical analysis of the market liquidity. Table 4.1 shows the statistical result, XML1 and XML2 represent the market liquidities. Figure 4.1 is the market liquidity's actual fluctuation diagram in 2018, the abscissa represents the time and the ordinate represents the liquidity index.

Table 4.1   Descriptive statistics on the liquidity of the new OTC Market

	Mean	S. D	Skew	Kurt	J – B	P
XML1	0.065	0.027	3.033	20.730	3555.59 *	0.0000
XML2	3.884	2.009	2.509	12.961	1259.61 *	0.0000

Note: Symbols "S. D", "Skew", "Kurt" is Std. Dev, Skewness, and Kurtosis respectively. "J – B" denotes statistic tests for the null hypothesis of normality in sample returns distribution. ∗ Indicates significance at the 1% significance level.

The descriptive statistics of two liquidity indexes are shown in Table 4.1. The skewness larger than 0, the values respectively are 3.033 and 2.509, which indicates that the time series of market liquidity is right – bias. The kurtosis larger than 3, the values respectively are 20.730 and 12.961. The J – B statistics reject the null hypothesis of Gaussian distribution at the 1% significance level indicating that all of the time series are fat－tailed. Therefore, the market liquidity in the new OTC market is fat－tailed.

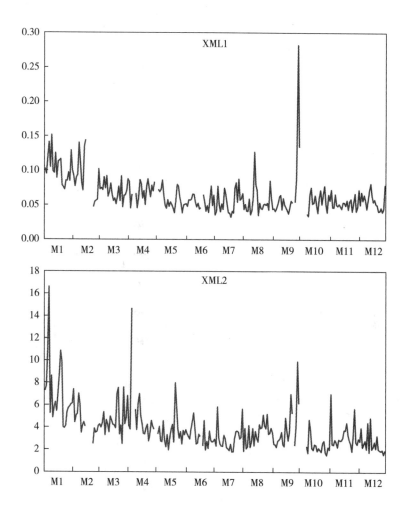

Figure 4.1   Liquidity fluctuation diagram of the new OTC market in 2018

4. 3. 2   Multifractal analysis

For the market liquidity series, we use the MF－DFA to analyze the nonlinear features. This method is to fit the time series of liquidity index to a local trend function for analysis, based on the MD – DFA method, where $int(0.25n) \geqslant s \geqslant l + 2$. This trend function could be a linear, quadratic, cubic, or higher – order polynomial. Generally, the higher – order is selected first for calculation. If the calculation results do not meet the conditional assumptions, then we calculate the results of the lower order polynomial. MF – DFA can not only identify whether the time series is linear or nonlinear, but also identify whether the series is single fractal or multifractal.

Through the above analysis, we consider that the local trend function of liquidity is a quadratic polynomial, use the MF – DFA to analyze nonlinear features of the market liquidity in the new OTC market and the large – cap market. Figure 4.2 shows the generalized Hurst exponents $h(q)$ of the new OTC market and the large – cap market.

We can see from Figure 4.2, the generalized Hurst exponent $h(q)$ of market liquidity in the new OTC market is related to the change of q. Generally, when $|q| > 2$, the structure of q order moment structure tends to be stable, so we mainly consider the case of $q_{min} = -2$ and $q_{max} = 2$. We employ the measure, $\Delta h = h(-2) - h(2)$, to quantify the multifractal degree of market liquidity. The results are shown in Table 4.2, XML1 and LML1 represent the liquidity of the new OTC market and the large – cap market, respectively.

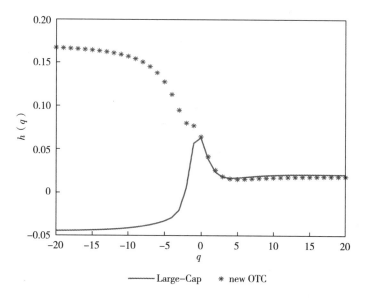

Figure 4. 2   Generalized Hurst exponent for quadratic polynomial

Table 4. 2   The multifractal degree of market liquidity for quadratic polynomial

	$h(-2)$	$h(2)$	$\Delta h = h(-2) - h(2)$
XML1	0. 080	0. 026	0. 055
LML1	0. 005	0. 024	-0. 018

Table 4. 2 shows the value of the generalized Hurst exponent $h(2)$ and $h(-2)$. For market liquidity of the large – cap market, the result of Δh does not meet the condition $\Delta h \geqslant 0$. In Figure 4. 2, there is a difference between two curves, the trends of two curves cannot compare the difference between the market liquidity in the new OTC market and the large – cap market. From Table 4. 2 and Figure 4. 2, we can see that using quadratic polynomial cannot meet calculation requirements.

Next, we calculate the linear polynomial and use MF – DFA to analyze the multifractal features of market liquidity in the new OTC market and large – cap market.

The results are shown in Table 4. 3 and Figure 4. 3. From Figure 4. 3, the market liquidity of the new OTC market and the large – cap market is multifractal.

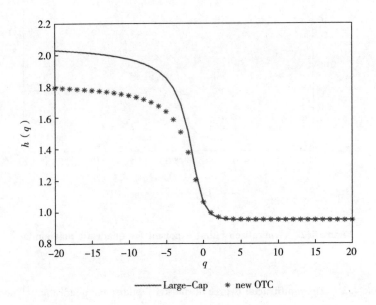

Figure 4. 3   Generalized Hurst exponent for linear polynomial

Table 4. 3   The multifractal degree of market liquidity for linear polynomial

	$h(-2)$	$h(2)$	$\Delta h = h(-2) - h(2)$
XML1	1. 378	0. 968	0. 410
LML1	1. 508	0. 963	0. 546

From Table 4. 3, the generalized Hurst exponent $h(2)$ of market liquidity in the new OTC market and the large – cap market larger than 0. 5, which indicates the market liquidity series is black noise sequences and long – range memory. From the degree of multifractality, compared the value of Δh between the new OTC market and the large – cap stocks, the market liquidity of the new OTC market is lower. The result indicates the liquidity complexity of the new OTC market is lower than that of the large – cap market. The reasons are that more mature trading system, low barriers for individual investors and high market participation. The higher market participation, the more frequent the market trade, and the greater the degree of liquidity's multi-fractality. Due to the special trading system of the new OTC market, the market sets higher investment conditions and greater restrictions for individual investors. Because of fewer investors, the investors more likely to hold stocks for long periods and the short – term trading is reduced, which shows the insufficiency of investors' enthu-siasm.

4. 3. 3   Sources of multifractality

To analyze the possible multifractal sources of the market liquidity series, the liquidity time series is shuffled, then using the MF – DFA to calculate and analyze multifractal feature of shuffled time series. According to the multifractality, we define $h^T(q)$ as the generalized Hurst exponent of the shuffled market liquidity time series. Generally, this approach can identify two different types of sources for multifractality in time series: (I) multifractality due to different long – range correlations for small and large fluctuations and we call it correlated multifractal; (II) multifractality relat-ed to the fat – tailed probability distributions of variations and we call it distributed multifractal.

There are three cases: when $h(q) - h^T(q) = 0$, the values of $h(q)$ and $h^T(q)$ depend on q, the source for multifractality of market liquidity series is distribu-ted multifractal. When $h^T(q) = 0.5$, the source for multifractality of market liquidi-ty series is correlated multifractal. When the values of $h(q)$ and $h^T(q)$ depend on q, but $h(q) - h^T(q) \neq 0$, the source for multifractality of market liquidity series is distributed multifractal and correlated multifractal.

We suppose the local trend function is a linear polynomial, the generalized Hurst exponents of market liquidity series for shuffled data is shown in Figure 4. 4. From Figure 4. 4, the value of the generalized Hurst exponent $h^T(q)$ is related to the change of q , the image is a monotonic decreasing curve, which indicates the market liquidity time – series for shuffled data still is multifractal. To analyze the sources for the multifractality of market liquidity in the new OTC market, we compare the values of $h(2)$ and $h^T(2)$. The results are shown in Table 4. 4.

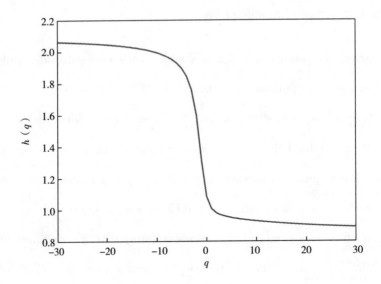

Figure 4. 4　Generalized Hurst exponent of the new OTC market for shuffled data

Table 4. 4　Generalized Hurst exponent of two kinds of series

	$h(2)$	$h^T(2)$	$h(2) - h^T(2)$
liquidity	0. 968	0. 979	− 0. 010

From Table 4.4, the generalized Hurst exponents $h(2)$ and $h^T(2)$ of market liquidity in the new OTC market both are greater than 0.5, which indicates that the market liquidity is persistence and long – term memory. The generalized Hurst exponents of original and shuffled series are different, $h(2) - h^T(2) \neq 0$, which shows that the source for multifractality of market liquidity in the new OTC market is caused by distributed multifractal and correlated multifractal.

Compared with the previous studies, we use MF – DFA to study the multifractal feature of market liquidity in China. We observe that market liquidity is persistence and long – term memory, besides the multifractality is caused by distributed multifractal and correlated multifractal.

4.3.4　Identification of the trended fluctuations

To ensure there are enough data samples for empirical research, we select ten companies the most trading Days in the new OTC market of 2018 to analyze, the results are shown in Table 4.5. We can see from Table 4.5 that there are differences between the mean values of the entropy dimension and the trend entropy dimension, which supports the above theoretical analysis. Simultaneously, for the change of the mean values of the entropy dimension and the trend entropy dimension, the mean value increases basically with the increase of the moving period, which roughly reflects that trend consistency of liquidity is more significant in the short term, trend reversion of liquidity is more significant in the long term.

According to the identification method and calculation results. To test the effectiveness of trend entropy dimension, we calculate the correct rate of trend entropy dimension identification. The correct rate is the most direct reflection of the trended fluctuation's identification, so we do the statistical test for the correct rate. The correct rate is that the moving tendency entropy dimension correctly identifies the ratio of the number of trended fluctuation stage to the market liquidity at a certain stage of trended fluctuation stage. If the market liquidity is at a certain stage of trended fluctuation times and this method correctly identified the trended fluctuation stage. So, it includes the number of identification errors and the number of times the trend entropy dimension does not recognize the trended fluctuation stage. Therefore, if the correct rate is significantly greater than 0.5, the results can avoid the existence of survival bias, which indicates that the identification method is effective.

However, to avoid the systemic errors in the identification process, we calculate the stochastic correct rate sequences of market liquidity. Systematic error means that the number of identification errors is very small, but the number of identification errors concentrated appears in the early stage. Hence it is difficult to directly use the correct rate to judge whether the tendency entropy dimension is accurate. We can improve the correct rate test by calculating the stochastic correct rate. Specifically, $\{x_{i_t}^k\}_{t=1}^{n_k}$ is the subsequence randomly selected in liquidity series $\{x_i\}_{i=1}^N$, assume $k \in [0,m]$ and $n_k \in (2,N]$, m is the number of times selected. For the liquidity subsequence $\{x_{i_t}^k\}_{t=1}^{n_k}$, assume the correct rate of identifying the trended fluctuation is p_k . Thus, we obtain the stochastic correct rate sequence $\{p_k\}_{k=1}^m$ of the liquidity series. If the stochastic correct rate sequence $\{p_k\}_{k=1}^m$ is significantly greater than 0.5, which indicates that using trend entropy dimension is effective and has no systematic errors in identifying trended fluctuations. Hence we randomly repeat 100 times to sample and calculate the stochastic correct rate sequence according to the results of each random sampling. At last, we take the T－test on the mean value of the stochastic correct rate sequences.

Table 4.5　Mean of moving trend entropy dimension and

moving entropy dimension sequence

		5days	10days	15days	20days	25days	30days
Rising entropy dimension	430208	1.037	1.179	1.258	1.279	1.301	1.319
	430493	1.112	1.217	1.322	1.322	1.346	1.404
	830899	1.074	1.205	1.316	1.284	1.360	1.411
	830978	1.085	1.177	1.313	1.290	1.353	1.373
	831129	1.050	1.213	1.293	1.274	1.313	1.355
	831550	1.067	1.215	1.255	1.295	1.295	1.355
	831562	1.067	1.192	1.265	1.285	1.329	1.342
	831628	1.061	1.194	1.271	1.284	1.331	1.376
	831900	1.093	1.233	1.264	1.328	1.348	1.366
	834793	1.075	1.182	1.307	1.270	1.329	1.330
Falling entropy dimension	430208	1.071	1.165	1.260	1.273	1.331	1.347
	430493	1.082	1.192	1.334	1.321	1.375	1.384
	830899	1.107	1.227	1.294	1.308	1.345	1.362
	830978	1.054	1.184	1.258	1.278	1.322	1.337
	831129	1.077	1.208	1.300	1.270	1.332	1.336
	831550	1.075	1.199	1.299	1.305	1.317	1.361
	831562	1.035	1.163	1.252	1.276	1.316	1.307
	831628	1.085	1.220	1.261	1.285	1.337	1.352
	831900	1.097	1.218	1.307	1.286	1.327	1.377
	834793	1.076	1.242	1.274	1.274	1.315	1.331
Entropy dimension	430208	1.278	1.310	1.383	1.352	1.389	1.409
	430493	1.313	1.360	1.431	1.396	1.437	1.455
	830899	1.303	1.345	1.427	1.392	1.434	1.454
	830978	1.281	1.315	1.405	1.375	1.422	1.446
	831129	1.293	1.327	1.401	1.366	1.407	1.420
	831550	1.314	1.324	1.397	1.369	1.410	1.435

Continued

		5days	10days	15days	20days	25days	30days
Entropy dimension	831562	1.292	1.321	1.382	1.353	1.388	1.409
	831628	1.307	1.313	1.384	1.358	1.397	1.420
	831900	1.315	1.337	1.413	1.380	1.421	1.433
	834793	1.308	1.330	1.398	1.374	1.411	1.429

The mean and T – test results are displayed in Table 4.6. From Table 4.6, under six different moving periods, the mean values of the stochastic correct rate sequences are significantly greater than 0.5 at 1% and 5% level. The test result indicates that the trend entropy dimension is effective for identifying the trended fluctuation of market liquidity. Using trend entropy dimension to identify trended fluctuation of market liquidity is good reference value and universality.

Table 4.6　The mean and T – test results of stochastic correct rate sequences

	5days	10days	15days	20days	25days	30days
430208	0.569 *	0.629 **	0.658 *	0.644 *	0.651 *	0.656 *
430493	0.649 *	0.672 *	0.677 *	0.658 **	0.661 *	0.672 *
830899	0.576 *	0.653 *	0.639 *	0.651 *	0.644 **	0.679 *
830978	0.564 *	0.666 *	0.663 *	0.617 *	0.664 *	0.670 **
831129	0.581 **	0.629 **	0.663 *	0.648 *	0.671 *	0.670 *
831550	0.584 *	0.660 *	0.681 *	0.664 *	0.633 **	0.665 *
831562	0.575 *	0.632 *	0.638 *	0.661 *	0.678 *	0.631 **
831628	0.586 *	0.631 *	0.646 *	0.645 *	0.646 *	0.653 *
831900	0.573 *	0.656 *	0.631 *	0.660 *	0.666 **	0.678 *
834793	0.589 **	0.654 *	0.666 *	0.649 *	0.659 *	0.662 *

Note： ** indicates significance at the 5% significance level. * indicates significance at the 1% significance leve.

Based on the above conclusions, the trend entropy dimension can identify trended fluctuations of liquidity effectively. At continuous upward stage or low reversal stage, the liquidity will go up in the later stage. At continuous downward stage or high reversal stage, the liquidity will fall in the later stage. Based on the effectiveness of the identification method, when the liquidity series is at continuous upward stage or low reversal stage, the market transaction can be carried out at the later period and the transaction cost will be reduced. At continuous downward stage and high reversal stage, the market transaction should be reduced to avoid losses caused by less liquidity and increased transaction cost in the later period.

4. 4　Robustness test

For the robustness of the results, we use the liquidity index that is calculated by method 2 and use the MF DFA to analyze the multiple features of liquidity in the new OTC market, identify the trended fluctuations of liquidity. The generalized Hurst exponent is shown in Figure 4. 5. From Figure 4. 5, the generalized Hurst exponents $h(q)$ of the liquidity in the new OTC market and the large – cap market are related to the change of q. $h(q)$ is a monotonic decreasing function of q. when $q < 0$, The changing trend of $h(q)$ value in the new OTC market is slower than that of the large – cap stocks, which indicates that the new OTC market is multifractal. Further, compare and analyze the liquidity multifractal degree of the new OTC market and the large – cap market. Table 4. 7 shows the results.

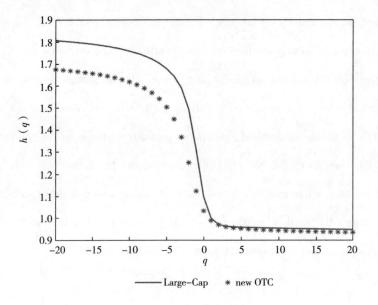

Figure 4. 5   Generalized Hurst exponent of market liquidity

Table 4. 7   Multifractal degree of liquidity for new

OTC Market and the large – cap market

	$h(-2)$	$h(2)$	$\Delta h = h(-2) - h(2)$
XML2	1. 252	0. 969	0. 282
LML2	1. 493	0. 971	0. 522

We can see from Table 4. 7, the generalized Hurst exponent $h(2) > 0.5$ of the liquidity in the new OTC market and the large – cap market, which indicates that the liquidity is sustainability and long – term memory. For the multifractal degree Δh, the multifractal degree of the market liquidity in the new OTC market is lower, indicates that the market liquidity complexity of the new OTC market is lower than that of the large – cap market. The two tests are consistent. Therefore, using the MF – DFA method to analyze the multifractal feature of market liquidity is robust.

The liquidity index of method 2 is used to identify trended fluctuations, and ten companies with the most trading time in the new OTC market are selected for analysis. The calculation results are as follows:

Table 4. 8　Mean of moving trend entropy dimension and moving entropy dimension sequence

		5days	10days	15days	20days	25days	30days
Rising entropy dimension	430208	1. 058	1. 211	1. 294	1. 266	1. 327	1. 327
	430493	1. 073	1. 182	1. 254	1. 304	1. 348	1. 372
	830899	1. 104	1. 209	1. 297	1. 325	1. 343	1. 401
	830978	1. 074	1. 202	1. 279	1. 274	1. 358	1. 352
	831129	1. 053	1. 186	1. 264	1. 256	1. 300	1. 345
	831550	1. 117	1. 179	1. 264	1. 269	1. 313	1. 335
	831562	1. 091	1. 202	1. 293	1. 316	1. 364	1. 370
	831628	1. 074	1. 202	1. 222	1. 270	1. 313	1. 344
	831900	1. 107	1. 203	1. 314	1. 316	1. 342	1. 385
	834793	1. 064	1. 205	1. 245	1. 257	1. 302	1. 322
Falling entropy dimension	430208	1. 089	1. 200	1. 297	1. 297	1. 358	1. 357
	430493	1. 062	1. 192	1. 291	1. 295	1. 328	1. 329
	830899	1. 107	1. 218	1. 331	1. 324	1. 367	1. 385
	830978	1. 110	1. 226	1. 273	1. 293	1. 338	1. 355
	831129	1. 047	1. 189	1. 273	1. 270	1. 334	1. 321
	831550	1. 040	1. 183	1. 269	1. 271	1. 311	1. 340
	831562	1. 088	1. 191	1. 277	1. 295	1. 328	1. 332
	831628	1. 018	1. 186	1. 262	1. 272	1. 308	1. 326
	831900	1. 119	1. 234	1. 325	1. 300	1. 345	1. 377
	834793	1. 090	1. 205	1. 277	1. 309	1. 325	1. 346
Entropy dimension	430208	1. 305	1. 327	1. 396	1. 368	1. 406	1. 424
	430493	1. 316	1. 337	1. 407	1. 371	1. 408	1. 421
	830899	1. 324	1. 346	1. 414	1. 388	1. 432	1. 456
	830978	1. 293	1. 328	1. 403	1. 376	1. 412	1. 427

Continued

		5days	10days	15days	20days	25days	30days
Entropy dimension	831129	1. 283	1. 305	1. 389	1. 356	1. 389	1. 412
	831550	1. 301	1. 313	1. 372	1. 354	1. 390	1. 412
	831562	1. 290	1. 325	1. 396	1. 369	1. 409	1. 425
	831628	1. 297	1. 301	1. 372	1. 345	1. 384	1. 405
	831900	1. 310	1. 342	1. 422	1. 389	1. 433	1. 458
	834793	1. 309	1. 336	1. 402	1. 370	1. 408	1. 424

According to the calculation results in Table 4. 8, the mean values of entropy dimension and trend entropy dimension of the selected stock liquidity are different; the mean values of entropy dimension and trend entropy dimension increase with the increase of the moving period, which is consistent with the calculation results of method 1 liquidity index. Besides, the mean and T – test results of stochastic correct rate sequences are calculated, and the results are shown in Table 4. 9.

Table 4. 9   The mean and T – test results of stochastic correct rate sequences

	5days	10days	15days	20days	25days	30days
430208	0. 570 *	0. 634 *	0. 684 *	0. 631 *	0. 656 *	0. 653 *
430493	0. 583 *	0. 648 *	0. 671 *	0. 654 *	0. 655 **	0. 687 *
830899	0. 578 *	0. 634 *	0. 653 *	0. 647 *	0. 647 *	0. 673 **
830978	0. 586 *	0. 638 *	0. 677 *	0. 637 *	0. 654 *	0. 676 *
831129	0. 550 *	0. 644 *	0. 644 **	0. 621 **	0. 667 *	0. 674 *
831550	0. 547 **	0. 609 **	0. 652 *	0. 638 *	0. 634 **	0. 651 *
831562	0. 580 *	0. 645 *	0. 669 *	0. 630 *	0. 655 *	0. 678 **
831628	0. 574 *	0. 652 *	0. 647 *	0. 651 *	0. 656 *	0. 648 *
831900	0. 592 **	0. 658 *	0. 669 *	0. 667 **	0. 662 *	0. 685 *
834793	0. 567 *	0. 655 *	0. 639 *	0. 626 *	0. 658 **	0. 639 **

Note： ** indicates significance at the 5% significance level. * indicates significance at the 1% significance level.

From the results, under six different moving periods, the mean values of the stochastic correct rate sequences are significantly greater than 0.5 at 1% and 5% level. The test result indicates that using the trend entropy dimension to identify trended fluctuations of market liquidity is robust.

4.5   Summary

In this study, we investigate the nonlinear feature of market liquidity in China's new OTC market. We select 990 listed companies in the new OTC market as a sample, use the MF – DFA method and the generalized Hurst exponent to analyze the liquidity's nonlinear feature, compare the multifractal degree of market liquidity in the new OTC market and the large – cap market. Meanwhile, to analyze the sources of market liquidity's non – linear in the new OTC market, we reset the liquidity time series to analyze the nonlinear feature, select 10 stocks in the new OTC market to identify the liquidity trended fluctuations by trend entropy dimension. We carry out the robustness test.

We find that: The market liquidity of the new OTC market is multifractal and the generalized Hurst exponent of market liquidity is related to the change of order. The first – order generalized Hurst exponent of market liquidity in the new OTC market and the large – cap market is between 0.5 and 1, which indicates that the liquidity of the two markets is sustainability and long – range memory. The liquidity multifractal degree of the new OTC market is lower than that of the large – cap market, which indicates that the complexity of market liquidity in the new OTC market is lower. The multifractality sources of market liquidity are the correlated multifractality and the distributed multifractality. The trend entropy dimension is validity and universality in identifying trended fluctuations of market liquidity.

According to the research results, we can know that the state should not only increase the support for small and medium – sized enterprises but also strengthen the supervision of the relevant stocks in the new OTC market, such as systemic financial risks and liquidity manipulation. Meanwhile, improving the market – related supporting system, establishing a multi – level and three – dimensional investment mechanism can effectively alleviate the financing difficulties of small and medium – sized enterprises.

Chapter 5　The Nonlinear Characteristics Analysis and Trend Identification of Liquidity in Chinese Stock Index Futures Markets

5. 1　Introduction

Liquidity is an important issue in the study of modern financial market. In the market with sufficient liquidity, investors can quickly complete the transaction at a lower cost. No matter how the demand of investors's orders changes, they can be met in time and will not cause great fluctuation to the market. On the contrary, if the market liquidity is poorer, it will lead investors's trading into difficulties, transaction costs soaring, serious shock on the market, and even lead to financial crisis. The core performance of the financial crisis is the sudden depletion of market liquidity. Under the influence of covid – 19, from February 24 to 28, 2020, the three major U. S. stock indexes all recorded the largest weekly decline since the 2008 financial crisis, with a decline of more than 10%. After that, the epidemic spread to the crude oil futures market, so that the price of U. S. crude oil futures (WTI) delivered in May plummeted by about 300% , even the first negative value in the history of futures trading occurred. These drastic market fluctuations are due to the short – term sudden depletion of liquidity caused by pessimistic market expectations. Therefore, in – depth study of market liquidity can not only maintain the stability of the market, but also improve the effective allocation of resource and promote the sustainable development of economy.

The study of financial market liquidity has a long history, but there is still no agreement on the definition of liquidity. In 1958, Tobin first proposed the concept of financial asset liquidity, and pointed out that when the seller wants to sell the asset as soon as possible, the possible loss is the standard to measure the asset liquidity. Black (1971) believes that when any number of securities in the market can be bought and sold at any time, it can be considered that the market has good liquidity. Pastor and Stambaugh (2003) defined liquidity as the ability to quickly complete a large number of transactions at low cost, without changing the price of securities. Borio (2004) believes that if the transaction can be completed quickly and has less impact on the price, the market liquidity is better. In addition, scholars also consider the selection of liquidity measurement indicators from multiple dimensions. Amihud and Mendelson (1986) found that there is a positive correlation between the expected return of assets and the bid ask spread, and the bid ask spread can be used as an indicator of liquidity. Kyle (2003) and Hasbrouck (2003) measured the liquidity index from the depth and width of the market respectively. Amihud (2002) used the ratio of absolute return rate to turnover as an indicator of illiquidity, and studied the relationship between liquidity and stock return. The study found that expected market

illiquidity has a positive impact on stock excess return.

In addition to the traditional security market, the financial derivative market is

also very important. As an important financial derivative, stock index futures have

the characteristic of two – way trading. Investors can not only choose the trading mode

of "buy before sell", but also choose "sell before buy". No matter which trading

mode is adopted, investors can obtain potential benefits by analyzing the changes of

stock index. Stock index futures is a sincreasingplement to the unilateral trading mode

of the stock market, and also an important part to improve and perfect the entire fi-

nancial system. Liquidity is an important reference index to measure the value of fu-

tures. This is because stock index futures, as the expected value of stock index, is

reflected by the form of futures contract. In order to ensure the fair and open price,

the exchange of information is very important, and high liquidity can transmit market

information in time and helps to discover the value of futures contracts. Liu (2005)

believes that the sharp decrease of futures liquidity will make it impossible to collect

market information through the futures market, and can not provide a fair and trans-

parent price for the market through the trading mechanism of open bidding. Li et al.

(2012) believe that after the introduction of CSI 300 index futures, the liquidity of

component stocks was strengthened, the price discovery ability is improved, and the

trading stability is improved. Zhang and Wei (2012) built a model of margin and

market liquidity. The study found that there is a negative relationship between margin

level and liquidity of stock index futures market. The increase of margin reduces vo-

lume of trading contracts and cause poorer futures liquidity. Zhou et al. (2015),

through studying the high – frequency data of CSI 300 index futures, found that the

probability of market informed trading has a significant predictive effect on the future liquidity of the market. When the probability of market informed trading is high, the future liquidity level of the market is low. Li and Guo (2017), through the analysis of high – frequency data of CSI 300 index and stock index futures, found that the futures – cash basis will lead to investors's carry trade and ultimately reduce the market liquidity, but after the index futures and short selling are limited, the futures – cash basis can not affect the market liquidity through arbitrage.

In fact, the index futures market is a complex system, which does not conform to the hypothesis of efficient market theory, and the complex changes of index futures liquidity are caused by many different dimensional factors. Therefore, the research on the liquidity of index futures needs to be considered from another perspective, especially the fractal theory. Compared with the efficient market hypothesis, fractal market theory can better explain the characteristics of the financial market. Peng et al. (1994) proposed detrended fluctuation analysis (DFA) to study the fractal characteristics of the market. Aiming at the disadvantage that this method can not be used to describe the multi – scale and fractal subsets of time series, kantelhardt et al. (2002) proposed multifractal detrended fluctuation analysis (MF – DFA), which uses multi – scale to describe the characteristics of different levels of the fractal market. Yin and Hua (2017) verified the non – linear characteristics of the stock market liquidity from a micro perspective through BDS test and Hurst exponent, which provides a new way to study the characteristics of the market liquidity. For the fractal characteristics of the futures market, Huang et al. (2013) found that there are multifractal characteristics in the volume – price relationship of China's metal futures market, and pointed out that the main reasons for the multifractal characteristics of the futures market are long – term memory and fat – tailed distribution. Wang and Suo (2014) used the multifractal detrended cross – correlation analysis (MF – X – DFA) to study the multifractal characteristics of China's index futures market and spot market, and the long – term cross correlation between the two markets. Tang and Zhu (2019) used high – frequency data to study that in each stage of bull and bear market, CSI 300 index futures has multifractal characteristics, and there are obvious differences in long memory and market risk in each stage. In order to describe the liquidity characteristics of the index futures market more accurately, this paper will use MF – DFA to analyze the nonlinear characteristics of futures liquidity, and analyze the multifractal degree of futures liquidity according to the generalized Hurst exponent.

In the real market, investors and regulators not only pay attention to the liquidity characteristics of index futures market, but also pay more attention to its fluctuation trend. The fluctuation prediction of futures liquidity can not only reduce the transaction cost of investors, but also provide early warning for the extreme change of liquidity. However, due to the nonlinear characteristics of the financial market, market tend not to fluctuate according to the normal distribution assumed by the efficient market hypothesis, and the relevant historical data also show that market fluctuation often has long – term correlation. Therefore, many scholars classify market fluctuation into two categories: one is that the fluctuation direction of the financial market is consistent with that of the previous moment (Gegadeesh and Titman); the other is that the fluctuation direction of the financial market reverses (Debond), which are called fluctuation trend consistency and trend contrarian respectively. After that, Bernstein (1993) combined the two fluctuation characteristics and put forward the concept of momentum life cycle and analyze the transformation relationship between two fluctuation characteristics. Galariotis (2014), Adam et al. (2016), Wu and Wang (2016) and other scholars have proved that there is a transformation relationship between trend consistency and trend contrarian in the stock market. At the same time, aiming at the nonlinear characteristics and complex structure of the futures market, it is not accurate to use simple autocorrelation analysis to study the fluctuation trend of futures liquidity. Mandelbrot (1999) and Xu (2011) believe that it is more realistic to construct a measurement of fluctuation trend recognition with nonlinear characteristics. Falconer (2003) proposed the entropy dimension based on the nonlinear theory, and used the entropy dimension to describe the fluctuation trend of time series. Then, Yan (2017) and Wu et al. (2018) used the trendrncy entropy dimension to effectively recognize the fluctuation trend of the stock market. Trendency entropy dimension is an improvement on the basis of entropy dimension recognition method, which can not only recognize the fluctuation characteristics of time series, but also recognize the direction of fluctuation trend. In order to accurately recognize the fluctuation trend of futures market liquidity, this paper uses the trendency entropy dimension to recognize the fluctuation trend of futures market liquidity, and tests the effectiveness of the method.

This paper uses the improved Amihud liquidity index to measure the liquidity of CSI 300 index futures. , aims at the current month contract, next month contract, inter season contract and next season contract, and uses the relevant trading data from April 16, 2010 to December 31, 2019 to analyze the non – linear characteristics of futures liquidity, the degree and cause of multifractal by using multifractal detrended fluctuation analysis (MF – DFA) and generalized Hurst exponent. In addition, combined with the nonlinear characteristics of futures liquidity, this paper uses the trendency entropy dimension method to recognize the fluctuation trend of futures liquidity, and tests the accuracy of trendency entropy dimension to recognize liquidity under seven mobile deadlines; then, uses the random accuracy rate to verify the effectiveness of the method; finally, performs a robustness test.

5. 2   Data description

5. 2. 1   Sample data

On April 16, 2010, China's financial futures trading launched the first index futures – CSI 300 index futures. This index futures are the earliest in the current China's financial futures, and the underlying stocks are also the most representative enterprises in China's stock market. As the index futures target, the CSI 300 index is composed of 300 stocks with the largest scale and the best liquidity in the Shanghai and Shenzhen stock markets. The sample interval selected in this paper is from April 16, 2010 to December 31, 2019, with a total of 2,363 daily indicators. Because the futures market has different contracts in trading every day, according to the length of holding period, these can be divided into four categories: current month contract, next month contract, inter season quarter contract and next season contract. The holding period of the current month contract is the shortest, followed by next month contract and inter season contract, and the holding period of next season contract is the longest. All data are from RESSET database.

5. 2. 2   Liquidity indexes

Method 1: the index uses the ratio of daily highest price and lowest price, which is an improvement on Amihud illiquidity index. The calculation formula is as follows:

$$L_t^1 = \ln(1 + Vol_t/V_t) \tag{5.1}$$

Thereinto, Vol_t represents the trading volume of CSI 300 futures contract in the day t, V_t represents the fluctuation of CSI 300 futures contract in the day t, $V_t = \ln(P_{High,t}/P_{Low,t})$, $P_{High,t}$ and $P_{Low,t}$ represents the highest price and lowest price of the contract respectively.

Method 2: considering the actual situation of the futures market, the number of contracts traded every day can also reflect the liquidity of the futures market. At the same time, in order to avoid large fluctuations in the data, this paper uses the logarithmic index of contract transactions to construct another liquidity index.

$$L_t^2 = \ln(Vol_t) \tag{5.2}$$

Thereinto, Vol_t represents the trading volume of CSI 300 futures contracts in the day t. In this paper, the liquidity index calculated by this method is used as the index of robustness test.

5.3　Empirical research

5.3.1　Descriptive statistic

In order to preliminarily verify the nonlinear characteristics of the liquidity of CSI 300 index futures, this paper calculates the kurtosis, skewness and J – B statistics of the liquidity series of current month contract, next month contract, and next season contract respectively, so as to intuitively judge whether the liquidity of futures has nonlinear characteristics. Table 1 lists the liquidity mean, kurtosis, skewness and

J – B statistics of the four futures contracts from April 16, 2010 to December 31, 2019, using liquidity indicators L^1. At the same time, Table 5. 2 lists the descriptive statistics of liquidity indicators L^2 in the same time range. Finally, Figure 5. 1 and Figure 5. 2 show the futures liquidity series chart drawn by the two liquidity indicators.

It can be seen from Table 5. 1. The standard deviation of the current month contract and the next month contract is greater than that of the inter season contract and the next season contract, which indicates that the liquidity fluctuation of the current month contract and the next month contract with shorter holding period is larger. The skewness of contract liquidity in the current month is – 0. 1, showing the characteristics of left skewness, while the skewness of the other three contracts is all positive, showing obvious right skewness; the kurtosis of the four contracts is less than the standard of normal distribution, not in line with the characteristics of normal distribution. For the J – B statistics, the J – B statistics of the liquidity of the four contracts do not meet the characteristics of normal distribution, and a p value of zero means that the liquidity time series rejects the original hypothesis, which indicates that the liquidity time series of the four contracts do not meet the normal distribution assumption of the efficient market hypothesis. Therefore, the liquidity of CSI 300 index futures is significantly non normal distribution. At the same time, the descriptive statistical results of liquidity indicators in Table 5. 2 are similar to those in Table 5. 1, which shows that the liquidity of index futures does not meet the normal distribution assumption of efficient market hypothesis under these two indicators.

Table 5.1   Descriptive statistics on liquidity of CSI 300 index futures (L^1)

Contract type	Mean value	Standard deviation	Skewness	Kurtosis	JB statistics	P value
Current month contract	15.667	1.591	−0.100	1.674	177.067	0.000
Next month contract	13.225	1.889	0.164	2.790	14.898	0.000
Inter season contract	12.301	1.410	0.184	2.376	51.645	0.000
Next season contract	10.606	1.276	0.260	2.842	29.039	0.000

Table 5.2   Descriptive statistics on liquidity of CSI 300 index futures (L^2)

Contract type	Mean value	Standard deviation	Skewness	Kurtosis	JB statistics	P value
Current month contract	11.533	1.703	−0.018	1.617	188.382	0.000
Next month contract	9.094	1.962	0.212	2.734	24.765	0.000
Inter season contract	8.166	1.498	0.448	2.527	101.103	0.000
Next season contract	6.442	1.354	0.638	3.276	167.568	0.000

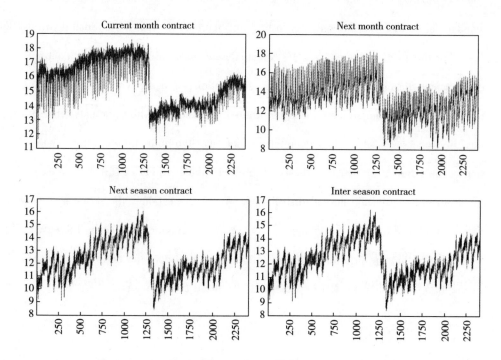

Figure 5.1   CSI 300 index futures liquidity time series (L^1)

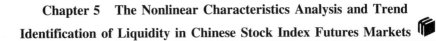
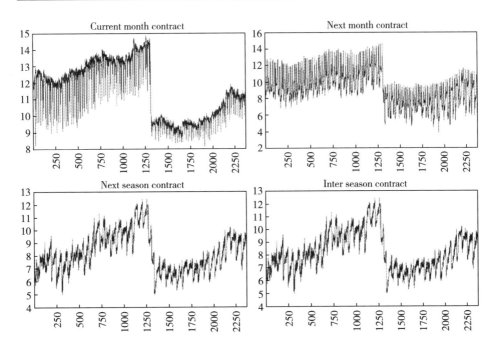

Figure 5. 2　CSI 300 index futures liquidity time series (L^2)

5. 3. 2　Multifractal characteristics test of liquidity

This part makes an empirical test on the multifractal characteristics of the liquidity of CSI 300 index futures. By using liquidity index L^1 , futures contracts are divided into four categories according to the holding period, namely current month contract, next month contract, inter season contract and next season contract. The sample range is from April 16, 2010 to December 31, 2019. MF – DFA is used to fit the time series of futures liquidity into a trend function, assuming that the trend function is a first order polynomial.

Figure 5. 3 shows the multifractal characteristics of the liquidity of four futures contracts. The ordinate is the value of $h(q)$, and the abscissa is the value of q . In function $h(q) \sim q$ image of four futures contract liquidity, the value of $h(q)$ changes with q, and presents a monotonic decreasing trend, in which the curve representing the current month contract changes the most, and the curve representing the next season contract changes the least. According to MF – DFA method, in the function $h(q) \sim q$ of time series, when the value of $h(q)$ is a variable related with q, the time series has multifractal characteristics. Therefore, it can be seen from the trend in Figure 5. 3 that the liquidity of four futures contracts has multifractal characteristics.

In order to measure the multifractal degree of liquidity, the q order moment structure tends to be stable when the value of q is greater than 2 or less than -2, and the value of $h(2)$ is the generalized Hurst exponent obtained by the classical R/s method. Therefore, the multifractal degree of liquidity can be calculated according to the formula $\Delta h = h(-2) - h(2)$. Table 3 shows the multifractal degree of liquidity of four futures contracts. It can be seen from Table 5. 3 that Δh of the four contracts are greater than 0. 5, which indicates that the liquidity of futures contracts has persistence and long – term memory. A higher Δh indicates a stronger degree of multifractality of liquidity, In Table 3, Δh of contract liquidity of current month with the shortest holding period is the largest, reaching 0. 915, while Δh of contract liquidity of the next season with the longest holding period is the smallest, only 0. 511, and Δh decreases with the increase of the holding period of the contract, which indicates that the longer the holding period of the CSI 300 index futures contract is, the lower the degree of multifractal of the futures contract liquidity is. Therefore, the liquidity market risk and extreme risk of short – term futures contracts are greater than other long – term contracts. With the increasing holding period, the liquidity market risk and extreme risk of futures will gradually decrease. It can be seen from RESSET database that during the period from April 16, 2010 to December 31, 2019, the average daily trading volume of contracts in the current month is 319759, the average daily trading volume of contracts in the next month is 59194, the average daily trading volume of contracts in the inter season is 11687, and the average daily trading volume of contracts in the next season is 1988. When the holding period of futures contract increases, the average daily trading volume of the contract will decrease. The current month contract with the shortest holding period has the most frequent transactions among the four futures contracts. In the futures market, investors tend to trade short – term futures contracts. Frequent trading of investors leads to more complex changes in futures liquidity. The increase of trading volume makes the market risk and extreme risk of liquidity gradually increase. With the increase of the holding period of the contract, the volume of transactions of investors gradually decreases, and the complexity of futures liquidity decreases, so Δh of futures contract liquidity will decrease with the increase of the holding period.

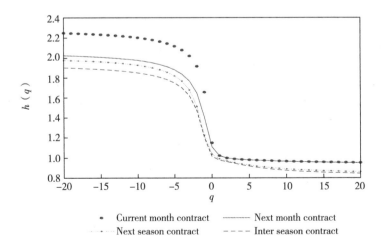

Figure 5. 3   Multifractal characteristics of four futures contracts

Table 5. 3   Multifractal dimensions of four contract liquidity

Contract type	$h(-2)$	$h(-1)$	$h(0)$	$h(1)$	$h(2)$	Δh
Current month contract	1. 914	1. 656	1. 150	1. 022	0. 999	0. 915
Next month contract	1. 647	1. 406	1. 110	1. 021	0. 999	0. 648
Inter season contract	1. 514	1. 225	1. 037	0. 991	0. 969	0. 546
Next season contract	1. 473	1. 201	1. 015	0. 977	0. 961	0. 511

5. 3. 3   Analysis of the causes of multifractal liquidity

From the previous part of the study, we can see that the liquidity of China's index futures market has obvious multifractal characteristics. However, what is the reason that this multifractal feature exists in the index futures market? This part will analyze the possible reasons from the perspective of time series. Firstly, the liquidity time series of futures contracts are randomly scrambled, so that there is no correlation between adjacent time nodes. Then, MF – DFA method is used to calculate and analyze the multifractal characteristics of the resetting liquidity series. The multifractal characteristics of the resetting liquidity series are shown in Figure 5. 4. It can be seen from Figure 5. 4 that after the time series of futures liquidity is randomly scrambled, $h^T(q)$ changes with the value of q , and the function $h^T(q) \sim q$ is a decreasing function, indicating that the liquidity series after reset still has multifractal characteristics.

According to the multifractal correlation theory, if $h^T(q) = q$, $h(q)$ and $h^T(q)$ all change with q , the multifractal formation of the original time series is only caused by the distribution multifractal; if $h^T(q) \neq q$, $h(q)$ and $h^T(q)$ all change with q , the multifractal characteristics of liquidity are caused by both the correlation multifractal and the distribution multifractal. Because the value of $h(2)$ is the generalized

Hurst exponent obtained by R/s method, in order to analyze the multifractal causes of liquidity in futures market, table 5 lists the values of $h(2)$ and $h^T(2)$ before and after liquidity reset. It can be seen from Table 5.5 that the generalized Hurst exponentes of liquidity series before and after reset are all greater than 0.5, the liquidity of four futures contracts are persistent and long – term memory, and the generalized Hurst exponentes before and after reset are not equal, which meets the conditions $h^T(q) \neq h(q)$. At the same time, Figures 5.3 and Figure 5.4 also prove that $h(q)$ and $h^T(q)$ changes with the change of q. The results show that the multifractal causes of liquidity of CSI 300 index futures are correlation multifractal and distribution multifractal.

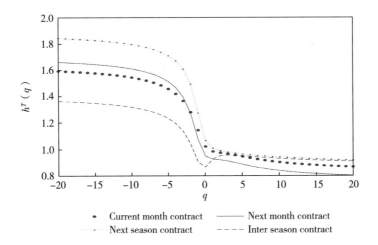

Figure 5.4   Multifractal characteristics of resetting liquidity series

5.3.4   Identification of fluctuation trend

Trendency entropy dimension is a nonlinear time series fluctuation trend recognition

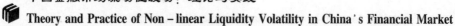
Table 5.4   Analysis of the multifractal characteristics causes of future contract liquidity

Contract type	$h(2)$	$h^T(2)$	$h(2) - h^T(2)$
Current month contract	0.999	0.975	0.024
Next month contract	0.999	0.921	0.078
Inter season contract	0.969	0.990	−0.022
Next season contract	0.961	0.953	0.009

method. Because the liquidity of CSI 300 index futures has nonlinear characteristics, this paper uses this method to recognize the liquidity fluctuation trend of four futures contracts. 5 Days, 10 Days, 30 Days, 60 Days, 90 Days, 120 Days and 240 Days are selected as the moving periods. The liquidity entropy dimension series and trendency entropy dimension series of four futures contracts are calculated under these seven moving periods. The trendency entropy dimension divides the time series into the increasing range and the decreasing range, and calculates the entropy dimensions of the time series in the two ranges, which are called the increasing entropy dimension and the decreasing entropy dimension respectively. The general entropy dimension does not distinguish the increasing and decreasing range, but calculates the entropy dimension of all time series. Due to the length, this section only lists the mean value of each dimension. Table 5.5 is the mean value of increasing entropy dimension of futures liquidity, table 6 is the mean value of decreasing entropy dimension of futures liquidity, and Table 5.7 is the mean value of entropy dimension of futures liquidity.

From the statistical results in Table 5.5 to Table 5.7, although the moving period is the same, the mean value of the entropy dimension and the trendency entropy dimension of liquidity are not equal. In addition, the mean values of the three entropy dimension series generally increase with the increase of moving periods, which indicates that the trend consistency of futures liquidity is more significant in the short term, and the trend reversal is more significant in the long term. The test results show that there is no trend reversal in the liquidity of futures contracts, and the liquidity of CSI 300 index futures only has the trend consistency of maintaining the fluctuation characteristics of the previous time node, and does not have trend reversal.

Table 5. 5   Mean value of increasing entropy dimension of four futures contract liquidity

Contract type	5 Days	10 Days	30 Days	60 Days	90 Days	120 Days	240 Days
Current month contract	1. 072	1. 190	1. 304	1. 366	1. 382	1. 419	1. 469
Next month contract	1. 100	1. 162	1. 233	1. 305	1. 305	1. 339	1. 406
Inter season contract	1. 110	1. 206	1. 273	1. 330	1. 350	1. 367	1. 422
Next season contract	1. 106	1. 203	1. 308	1. 359	1. 368	1. 393	1. 436

Table 5. 6   Mean value of decreasing entropy dimension of four futures contract liquidity

Contract type	5 Days	10 Days	30 Days	60 Days	90 Days	120 Days	240 Days
Current month contract	1. 102	1. 197	1. 330	1. 380	1. 390	1. 431	1. 470
Next month contract	0. 877	1. 016	1. 199	1. 239	1. 253	1. 294	1. 379
Inter season contract	1. 072	1. 182	1. 349	1. 398	1. 385	1. 382	1. 411
Next season contract	1. 088	1. 197	1. 349	1. 399	1. 388	1. 403	1. 434

Table 5. 7   Mean liquidity entropy dimension of four futures contracts

Contract type	5 Days	10 Days	30 Days	60 Days	90 Days	120 Days	240 Days
Current month contract	1. 305	1. 317	1. 384	1. 424	1. 437	1. 471	1. 515
Next month contract	1. 261	1. 238	1. 253	1. 317	1. 340	1. 388	1. 453
Inter season contract	1. 307	1. 315	1. 365	1. 380	1. 396	1. 419	1. 454
Next season contract	1. 313	1. 315	1. 388	1. 408	1. 417	1. 437	1. 468

5. 3. 5　Recognition validity test

In this paper, we use the trendency entropy dimension model to analyze the trend of future liquidity fluctuation, and get the relevant conclusions, which also has practical significance and application value. However, how accurate is this model and whether it can meet the daily needs of investors. Therefore, it is necessary to further verify the effectiveness of the trendency entropy dimension recognition method, and the recognition correct rate is the most direct reflection of the recognition effectiveness. In this part, the validity of recognizeing liquidity fluctuation trend is tested by recognition correct rate, which is the proportion of correct identification times to the total identification times. In order to avoid the survivorship bias of data, the effectiveness of the recognition method can be approved when the recognition correct rate is greater than 0. 5.

Table 5. 8　Correct rate of fluctuation trend recognition of futures liquidity

Contract type	5 Days	10 Days	30 Days	60 Days	90 Days	120 Days	240 Days
Current month contract	0. 567	0. 634	0. 647	0. 653	0. 648	0. 653	0. 675
Next month contract	0. 571	0. 624	0. 626	0. 595	0. 590	0. 618	0. 660
Inter season contract	0. 589	0. 644	0. 664	0. 658	0. 650	0. 641	0. 661
Next season contract	0. 583	0. 645	0. 662	0. 660	0. 658	0. 655	0. 671

Table 5. 8 shows the recognition correct rate of the trendency entropy dimension of futures liquidity. It can be seen from Table 5. 8 that under different moving periods, the recognition correct rate of the fluctuation trend of liquidity of four futures contracts is greater than 0. 5. Specifically, the average recognition correct rate in Table 5. 8 is 0. 636. Under the same moving period, the maximum range of recognition

correct rate of four futures contract liquidity is 0. 063. Therefore, this paper uses the trendency entropy dimension to recognize the fluctuation trend of futures liquidity, which is effective and universal.

5. 3. 6　Random accuracy test

It has been analyzed that the trendency entropy dimension is effective and universal to recognize the fluctuation trend of futures liquidity. This part considers that there may be systematic errors in the recognition process. Systematic error refers to that in the process of recognition, although the number of error recognition is small, the error recognition may be concentrated in a certain period of time. Although the final recognition correct rate is greater than 0. 5, the continuous error recognition in a certain period of time may lead to the final recognition correct rate is not representative. Therefore, in order to avoid such errors, this section improves the statistical method of recognition correct rate. The given time series $\{x_i\}_{i=1}^N$ are randomly extracted, $\{x_{i_t}^k\}_{t=1}^{n_k}$ are the subseriess extracted from the time series $\{x_i\}_{i=1}^N$, with a total of m times, $k \in [0,m]$, $n_k \in (2,N]$; for the liquidity random series $\{x_{i_t}^k\}_{t=1}^{n_k}$, assume that the correct rate of the trendency entropy dimension to recognize the fluctuation trend of the random series is p_k, so as to obtain the random correct rate $\{p_k\}_{k=1}^m$ of the original time series $\{x_i\}_{i=1}^N$. Therefore, if the accuracy rate $\{p_k\}_{k=1}^m$ of random time series is significantly higher than 0. 5, it can show that the trendency entropy dimension is effective in recognizeing the fluctuation trend stage of the original time series, and it can also show that there is no systematic error in recognizeing the fluctuation trend stage of the original time series. In this paper, we test the correct rate of each contract under different moving periods, and each test is randomly selected for

100 times. Finally, T – test is carried out on the mean value of random correct rate series of futures contract liquidity under different moving periods, the results are as follows:

Table 5.9   Mean value and T test results of random correct rate series

Contract type	5 Days	10 Days	30 Days	60 Days	90 Days	120 Days	240 Days
Current month contract	0.566 ***	0.646 ***	0.648 ***	0.653 **	0.649 ***	0.652 **	0.676 ***
Next month contract	0.571 ***	0.628 **	0.625 ***	0.595 ***	0.590 ***	0.618 ***	0.658 ***
Inter season contract	0.588 **	0.665 ***	0.664 ***	0.656 ***	0.649 ***	0.641 ***	0.662 ***
Next season contract	0.583 ***	0.661 ***	0.661 **	0.660 ***	0.659 ***	0.654 **	0.671 **

Note: ** indicates the significance level of 5% ; *** indicates the significance level of 1%.

It can be seen from Table 5.9 that under different moving periods, the random correct rate series of trend recognition pass the T – test at the significance levels of 1% and 5%, and the mean value of the random correct rate series of four different futures liquidity is significantly greater than 0.5. The results show that using the trendency entropy dimension to recognize the fluctuation trend of liquidity is effective and avoids the occurrence of systematic errors. This recognition method has good reference value and universality for the recognition of fluctuation trend of liquidity.

To sum up, whether using the critical value of recognition correct rate greater than 0.5 or T – test of random correct rate, the results show that the trendency entropy dimension can more accurately recognize the fluctuation trend of futures liquidity, and it is an effective measure to recognize the fluctuation trend of nonlinear time series. Thereinto, the recognition correct rate of four different futures liquidity pass T – test, which also shows that the trendency entropy dimension has robustness and universality in recognizeing the fluctuation trend of futures liquidity.

5. 4　Robustness test

For the test of multifractal characteristics of futures liquidity, in order to verify the robustness of the experimental results, this section will use the liquidity index of method 2, and use MF – DFA method to analyze the multifractal characteristics of four futures contract liquidity. The multifractal structure is shown in Figure 5. 5. It can be seen from Figure 5. 5 that the value of the generalized Hurst exponent of futures liquidity order is closely related to the value of, which is a monotonic decreasing function of. Moreover, the value of contract liquidity in the month with short holding period changes more than other types of contracts. At the same time, Table 5. 10 lists the multifractal dimensions of the liquidity of the four futures contracts, and further compares and analyzes the complexity of the multifractal dimensions of the liquidity of the four futures contracts. It can be seen from Table 5. 10 that the generalized Hurst exponent of the liquidity of the four futures contracts is greater than 0. 5, indicating that the liquidity of the futures contracts has the characteristics of persistence and long – term memory. From the multifractal dimension, the multifractal dimension of the current month contract with shorter holding period is higher, which indicates that the complexity of the liquidity of the contract is higher than that of other types of contracts, and the multifractal degree of futures liquidity decreases with the increase of holding period of futures contract. These results are consistent with the liquidity index calculation results of method 1. Therefore, this paper uses MF – DFA method to analyze the multifractal characteristics of futures liquidity, which has good robustness.

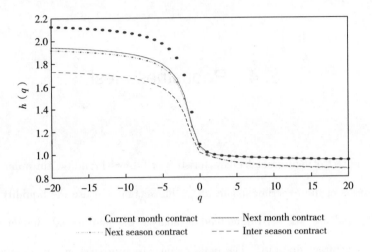

● Current month contract ——— Next month contract

············ Next season contract – – – – Inter season contract

Figure 5. 5　Multifractal characteristics of the four futures contracts

Table 5. 10　Multifractal dimensions of four contract liquidity

Contract type	$h(-2)$	$h(-1)$	$h(0)$	$h(1)$	$h(2)$	Δh
Current month contract	1. 695	1. 370	1. 088	1. 019	0. 998	0. 698
Next month contract	1. 517	1. 258	1. 073	1. 018	0. 997	0. 519
Inter season contract	1. 488	1. 242	1. 063	0. 999	0. 971	0. 517
Next season contract	1. 353	1. 153	1. 019	0. 988	0. 969	0. 384

5. 5　Summary

Liquidity, as the focus of the financial theory and real investment, is the core premise to judge the market. This paper uses the improved Amihud liquidity index to measure the liquidity of CSI300 index futures. According to the holding period of futures contracts, it is divided into four kinds of contracts: current month contract, next month contract, inter season contract and next season contract. The sample range is from April 16, 2010 to December 31, 2019. Based on the nonlinear characteristics of the financial market, this paper analyzes the nonlinear characteristics of futures liquidity and the degree and causes of multifractality by using MF – DFA and generalized Hurst exponent. In addition, combined with the non – linear characteristics of futures liquidity, this paper uses the trendency entropy dimension method to recognize the fluctuation trend of futures liquidity, and detects the accuracy of the trendency entropy dimension to recognize liquidity under seven moving periods. In order to avoid systematic error, this paper uses random correct rate to verify the effectiveness of the method. Finally, the robustness test is carried out. The results show that: MF – DFA verifies that the liquidity of CSI 300 index futures not only has nonlinear characteristics, but also has multifractal characteristics; The value $h(q)$ of generalized Hurst exponent changes with the order, and the value of $h(2)$ of four futures contracts liquidity ranges from 0.5 to 1, which proves that the liquidity of futures has nonlinear characteristics of persistence and long – term memory; The multifractal degree of liquidity of short – term current contract liquidity is higher than that of other futures contracts, which indicates that the liquidity complexity of current month contract is higher than that of other futures contracts. With the increase of holding period of futures contract, the multifractal degree of liquidity gradually decreases, so the liquidity complexity of short – term contract is higher than that of long – term contract. According to the average daily trading volume of futures contracts, the shorter the holding period, the larger the average daily trading volume of futures contracts. Frequent market transactions of investors increase the complexity of liquidity fluctuation, and increase the market risk and extreme risk of futures liquidity. Therefore, the regulatory authorities need to focus on strengthening the supervision of short – term contract transactions, and pay attention to the liquidity changes of long – term contracts; The trendency entropy dimension can recognize the fluctuation trend of futures liquidity in different stages, and the recognition correct rate and random correct rate test prove the effectiveness and universality of this method.

The results of this paper not only provide reference for investment decisions and reduce the risk of futures investment, but also provide suggestions for relevant departments to supervise the market risk and extreme risk of futures liquidity, which is good at the improvement of market supervision system and further strengthen the role of futures market in avoiding spot risk.

Chapter 6 Non – linear Volatilization Characteristics and Trend Identification of Liquidity in Chinese Crude Oil Futures Market

6. 1 Introduction

Crude oil is one of the most important strategic resources in the world and occupies a significant position in the international energy market; it is also a fundamental resource related to national security and people's livelihood development. Affected by the COVID – 19 and the breakdown of the OPEC + production reduction agreement, the global crude oil trading market is in deep recession. On April 20, WTI crude futures for May delivery tumbled by 309. 63% to – 37. 63 dollars per barrel, falling to a negative value for the first time in history. When the price of crude oil futures reached a negative value, many investors exclaimed: "Are crude oil futures worthless?"

In fact, one of the most fundamental reasons why the crude oil futures reached a negative value was the sudden lack of liquidity, namely the abnormal fluctuation of liquidity. The liquidity is the ability to quickly complete a large number of transactions at a lower cost without changing asset prices (Pastor and Stambaugh, 2003 ; Albuquerque et al. , 2020) . If the market liquidity is high, the investors can quickly complete the transaction at a low cost when they buy or sell orders, and this transaction will not make much difference to the market price. On the contrary, if the liquidity is insufficient, the investor's order will be traded at a higher price, or even untradeable situations will arise.

As the market closed on the afternoon of April 20, because the WTI crude futures for May delivery was approaching, many speculators or investors who had no demand for crude oil commodities began to cash out. Due to the sluggish international crude oil demand and other factors, the orders to be sold of crude oil futures increased while the orders to be bought decreased significantly. In other words, the buyer's liquidity of futures contracts suddenly dried up. This phenomenon directly prevented many futures contracts in the market from being sold at the predetermined prices, so the seller's quotation fell again and again, finally closing at a negative value. It is noted that that crude oil futures are still valuable. However, it is these factors such as inventory, transportation and actual market demand that make the sellers of futures contracts lack liquidity in a short period of time. Therefore, it is of important practical value and theoretical significance to study the liquidity of crude oil futures market.

Liquidity has been widely studied and applied in the securities market and futures market. Jacoby et al. (2000) and Xu et al. (2019) explored the influence of liquidity on stock price fluctuations and futures price fluctuations. In the crude oil market, Batten et al. (2019) also pointed out that liquidity plays a highly important role in crude oil market pricing. Liquidity is an important indicator to measure market operation, as well as an important reference to measure the value of futures contracts. Crude oil futures, as an expectation of the crude oil market value, are embodied in the form of futures contracts. To ensure the fairness and openness of prices, the exchange of information is essential. High liquidity can timely transmit market information and help discover the value of futures contracts. Some scholars have studied the risk aversion and diversification of Brent and WTI in the futures market and bulk commodity market (Maghyereh et al. , 2017; Sarwar et al. , 2018; Ma et al. , 2019). Pan et al. (2016) develops an asymmetric dynamic equi – correlation model to investigate the correlations between returns of petroleum futures and stock indices, finds that this model provides portfolios with better performances than existing popular methods, and energy price risk can be better hedged by stocks in oil – exporting countries than stocks in oil – importing countries. For the volatility of crude oil futures prices, Ma et al. (2018) found that short – term investors have a greater impact on the volatility of oil futures prices. Ji and Zhang (2018) analyzed the high – frequency data of INE crude oil futures prices and believed that there is a significant jump in market volatility.

The sudden short – term lack or abnormal fluctuations of liquidity indicate that liquidity is not subject to a random walk process under the efficient market hypothesis, but may have complex nonlinear characteristics. As a frontier theory of nonlinear science, fractal theory mainly adopts the principle of self – similarity and iterative generation to study some nonlinear problems in the market. For the financial market, the volatility of the financial market does not strictly follow the efficient market hypothesis (Grech, 2016; Han et al. , 2019; Wang and Wang, 2018; Bouoiyour et al. , 2018; Zhu and Zhang, 2018) . In order to investigate the characteristics of financial market volatility, Peters (1993) applied the fractal theory to the financial market and put forward the fractal market hypothesis (FMH) . On this basis, Peng et al. (1994) proposed the detrended fluctuation analysis (DFA) to study the fractal characteristics of financial market, but this method cannot be used to describe the multi – scale and fractal subsets of time series. Aiming at this problem, Kantelhardt et al. (2002) used multi – scale to describe different levels of the fractal market and proposed the multifractal detrended fluctuation analysis (MF – DFA) . Through the study of oil prices and energy stocks, Yang et al. (2016) found that the returns and volatility of energy industry indexes present obvious multifractal characteristics. Based on the comparison of the crude oil futures markets of INE, WTI and Brent, Wang et al. (2019) noticed that the multifractal characteristics of the INE crude oil futures market are weaker than those of the Brent crude oil futures market, and that the risk of the INE crude oil futures market is lower than that of mature crude oil futures markets, such as WTI and Brent.

For the commodity futures market, both parties to the transaction will not only pay attention to the volatility characteristics of market liquidity, but also give heed to the fluctuation trend of market liquidity in the future. If the trend of liquidity fluctuations can be accurately predicted, investors can effectively reduce transaction costs and increase investment returns. Meanwhile, the supervisory authority can also carry out key supervision of the market in advance to prevent drastic liquidity fluctuations. The trend of financial market fluctuations can generally be divided into trend consistency and trend reversion (Wu et al. , 2015; Moskowitz et al. , 2012; Shi and Zhou, 2017; Lim et al. , 2018) . For the stock market, if the stock price fluctuation is consistent with the previous period's stock price trend, the market fluctuation can be considered to show trend consistency (Subrahmanyam, 2018). Conversely, if the stock price trends of the two periods are different, the market fluctuation show trend reversion (Andrei and Cujean, 2017).

In summary, there are few researches on the nonlinear characteristics and trend prediction of crude oil futures market liquidity. To more accurately describe the liquidity characteristics and fluctuation trends of crude oil futures, and aimed at the deficiencies of using traditional autocorrelation analysis methods to study fluctuation trends, this paper will consider the complex structure of the crude oil futures market, explore the non－linear multifractal characteristics of liquidity in the INE, WTI and Brent crude oil futures markets using MF－DFA, compare and analyze the multifractal degree of liquidity based on the generalized Hurst exponent, and study the multifractal sources of the liquidity in the crude oil futures market. Finally, by the trend entropy dimension model, this paper will predict the fluctuation trend of crude oil futures market liquidity, and test the accuracy and effectiveness of the proposed method.

The remainder of the paper is organized as follows: Section 2 mainly focuses on the description of the method. Section 3 describes the data and index selection of liquidity in the crude oil futures market. Section 4 provides the empirical results, which include descriptive statistics of liquidity, multifractal analysis, sources of multifractality analysis, the identification of the trended fluctuations, and robustness test. Section 5 is the conclusion.

6. 2　Data description

6. 2. 1　Data of the sample

This paper selected the main continuous contracts of crude oil futures in WTI, Brent and INE, the sample period ranging from March 26, 2018 to June 30, 2020. For the selection of the moving period, 5, 10, 15, 30, 60, 90 and 120 Days were commonly used as the moving period. To ensure the reliability of the results, this paper selected all 7 types of moving periods and separately calculated the recognition accuracy rate during different moving periods.

6. 2. 2　Liquidity indicators

Method 1: This indicator used the ratio of the daily highest price to the lowest price, which was an improvement on the Amihud illiquidity indicator (Wang, 2013), and calculated as follows:

$$L_1 = \ln(1 + Vol_t / V_t) \tag{6.1}$$

Where Vol_t represented the trading volume of crude oil futures on the t day; V_t represented the volatility of futures contracts on the t day. $V_t = \ln(P_{High,t} / P_{Low,t})$, $P_{High,t}$ and $P_{Low,t}$ represented the highest and lowest prices of the futures contract, respectively.

Method 2: According to the actual situation of China's crude oil futures market, this paper used the improved Amivest liquidity ratio of Bai and Qin (2015), and constructed another liquidity indicator.

$$L_2 = \ln\left(\left| \frac{P_t \cdot Vol_t}{\frac{(P_t - P_{t-1})}{P_t}} \right| \right) \tag{6.2}$$

Where P_t represented the closing price of China's crude oil futures on the t day.

This paper used the liquidity index calculated by this method as the index of robust-

ness test.

6.3   Empirical analysis

6.3.1   Descriptive statistics

In order to preliminarily verify the fluctuation characteristics of liquidity in diffe-

rent crude oil futures markets, this paper calculated the standard deviation, kurtosis,

skewness, and J – B statistics of the two liquidity indicators to judge whether the fu-

tures liquidity meets the conditions of the efficient market hypothesis (EMH) . In

Table 6.1, we listed the mean, standard deviation, kurtosis, skewness and J – B sta-

tistics of the liquidity series in INE, WTI and Brent crude oil futures markets from

March 26, 2018 to June 31, 2020. Table 6.1 adopted L_1 liquidity index. At the

same time, we listed the descriptive statistics of L_2 liquidity index in Table 6.2. Fi-

gure 6.1 and Figure 6.2 demonstrated the liquidity fluctuation diagrams of WTI,

Brent and INE by two liquidity indicators respectively.

As shown in Table 6.1, the standard deviation of INE crude oil futures liquidity was larger than that of the other two crude oil futures markets, which indicated that the volatility of INE crude oil futures liquidity was larger than that of other mature crude oil futures markets such as WTI and Brent. The liquidity's skewness of WTI, Brent and INE crude oil futures reached -0.829, -0.777 and -0.966 respectively, suggesting that the liquidity of the three crude oil futures markets were all left – biased. The liquidity's kurtosis of WTI, Brent and INE crude oil futures reached 3.233, 3.884 and 3.225 respectively, all of which were larger than the kurtosis value of the standard normal distribution. This indicated that the liquidity of the three crude oil futures markets did not meet the requirements of the standard normal distribution. For J – B statistics, the J – B statistics of liquidity of the three crude oil futures markets did not meet the requirements of normal distribution and the probability value reached zero, indicating that the liquidity series rejected the null hypothesis and that the liquidity of the three crude oil futures markets did not conform to the normal distribution assumption of the efficient market hypothesis. Therefore, the liquidity of WTI, BRENT and INE crude oil futures markets was in significant non – normal distribution. In Table 6.2, the descriptive statistical results of Amivest liquidity indicators were similar to the conclusions of the Amihud indicators, suggesting that the liquidity of the three crude oil futures markets failed to meet the normal distribution assumption of the efficient market hypothesis.

Table 6.1　Descriptive statistics on the liquidity of different markets (L_1)

	Mean	Std. Dev.	Skewness	Kurtosis	Jarque – Bera	Probability
WTI	16.626	0.678	-0.829	3.233	62.850	0.000
BRENT	16.023	0.571	-0.777	3.884	73.307	0.000
INE	15.854	0.848	-0.966	3.225	87.061	0.000

Table 6.2　Descriptive statistics on the liquidity of different markets (L_2)

	Mean	Std. Dev.	Skewness	Kurtosis	Jarque – Bera	Probability
WTI	21.693	1.429	0.270	3.878	23.806	0.000
BRENT	21.207	1.359	0.452	3.917	38.024	0.000
INE	22.788	1.475	– 0.148	3.878	19.734	0.000

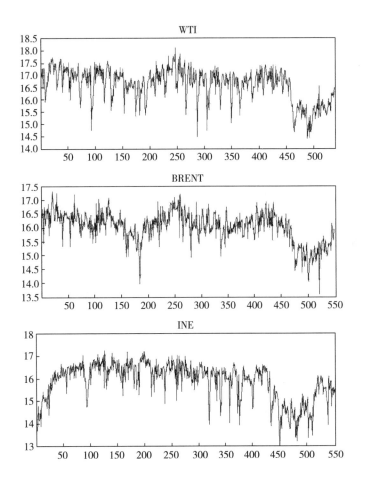

Figure 6.1　Liquidity fluctuation diagram of WTI, BRENT and INE (L_1)

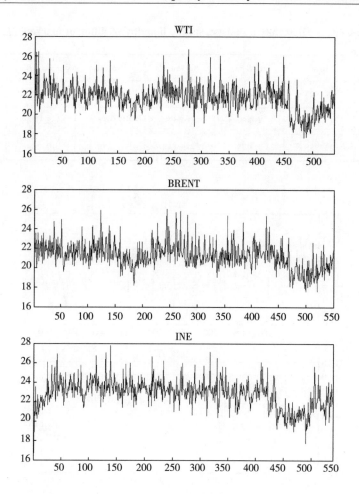

Figure 6. 2   Liquidity fluctuation diagram of WTI, BRENT and INE (L_2)

6. 3. 2   Multifractal analysis

In this section, we tested the multifractal characteristics of the crude oil futures liquidity, calculated the liquidity multifractal degree, and compared the multifractal complexity of liquidity in three crude oil futures markets. We used L_1 as the liquidity indicator, and the sample interval started from March 26, 2018 to June 31, 2020.

We adopted MF－DFA to fit the time series of crude oil futures liquidity into a trend function for calculation and assumed that the trend function was a first－order polynomial.

Figure 6.3 offered the generalized Hurst exponents of WTI, BRENT and INE crude oil futures liquidity. The ordinate represented the value of the generalized Hurst index $h(q)$, while the abscissa represented the value of the fluctuation function q. According to the MF－DFA, for the function $h(q) \sim q$ of the time series, when $h(q)$ was a variable related to the value of q, this meant that the time series had multifractal characteristics. Otherwise, the time series was a single fractal sequence and did not have multifractal characteristics. In Figure 6.3, the generalized Hurst exponent $h(q)$ of crude oil futures liquidity in the three markets changed with the change in q, and all three curves showed a monotonous decreasing trend. The results showed that the liquidity of WTI, BRENT and INE crude oil futures markets all had multifractal characteristics.

Although the liquidity of crude oil futures in WTI, BRENT and INE markets had multifractal characteristics, the change range of the liquidity's $h(q)$ in the three crude oil futures markets varied. In Figure 6.3, when $q < 0$, the $h(q)$ value of INE crude oil futures liquidity was the smallest, while the $h(q)$ value of WTI crude oil futures liquidity was the largest under the same conditions. In order to test the liquidity multifractal degree of crude oil futures, and according to the principle of MF－DFA, when $q > 2$ or $q < -2$, the structure of the q－order fluctuation function would tend to be stable. In addition, when $q = 2$, $h(2)$ was the value of the generalized Hurst exponent calculated by the R/S method. Therefore, the liquidity multifractal degree of crude oil futures in the three markets could be obtained by the calculation results based on formula $\Delta h = h(-2) - h(2)$.

Table 6. 3 presented the results of the liquidity multifractal degree in the WTI, BRENT and INE crude oil futures markets. The $h(2)$ values of liquidity in three crude oil futures markets were all larger than 0. 5, which indicated that the crude oil futures liquidity belonged to the black noise sequence characterized by persistence and long – term memory. Meanwhile, the larger the value of Δh, the stronger the multifractal degree of liquidity. As indicated by the results, the Δh value of INE crude oil futures liquidity reached the minimum of 0. 267, while the values of WTI and BRENT crude oil futures reached 0. 573 and 0. 488, respectively. Therefore, the INE crude oil futures had the lowest liquidity complexity. Compared with WTI and BRENT, the launch of China's crude oil futures was relatively late and there were fewer types of futures contracts. In addition, the average daily trading volume of INE crude oil futures arrived at 1. 237 million lots in the sample range, which was lower than that of WTI and BRENT (the average daily trading volume of WTI was 3. 392 million lots and that of BRENT was 1. 621 million lots). Due to the smaller trading volume, the trading frequency of crude oil futures also decreased, thus reducing the complexity of the transaction. Accordingly, the complexity of market liquidity was low, and the Δh value of liquidity was small, as shown by the results.

Table 6. 3　The multifractal degree of market liquidity in different markets

	$h(-2)$	$h(2)$	Δh
WTI	1. 559	0. 986	0. 573
BRENT	1. 475	0. 986	0. 488
INE	1. 254	0. 987	0. 267

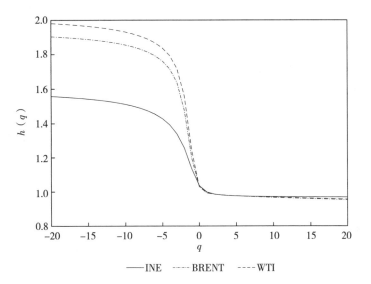

Figure 6. 3   Generalized Hurst exponent of market liquidity in different markets

6. 3. 3   Sources of multifractality

In this section, we mainly studied the sources of the liquidity multifractality in

three crude oil futures markets. According to the findings of the above section, the

liquidity in three crude oil futures markets all had multifractal characteristics, but the

multifractal degree varied. To analyze the possible sources of the liquidity's multifrac-

tality, we shuffled and reset the time series of crude oil futures liquidity, and then

used the MF－DFA to calculate the generalized Hurst exponent of shuffled liquidity

sequence. Finally, we compared the generalized Hurst exponents of the shuffled liq-

uidity sequence and the original liquidity sequence. We defined $h^{T}(q)$ as the genera-

lized Hurst exponent of the shuffled liquidity sequence. According to the principles of

multifractality, there were two sources of multifractality: (Ⅰ) correlated multifractal

caused by different long－range correlations for small and large fluctuations; (Ⅱ) distributed multifractal caused by fat – tailed probability distribution of fluctuations.

According to the calculation results, there existed three cases: ① If $h(q) - h^T(q) = 0$, $h(q)$ and $h^T(q)$ changed with the change in q, then the distributed multifractal was the cause of the liquidity multifractality; ②If $h^T(q) = 0.5$, then the correlated multifractal was the cause of the liquidity multifractality; ③ If $h(q) - h^T(q) \neq 0$, $h(q)$ and $h^T(q)$ changed with the change in q, then the liquidity multifractality was jointly caused by the correlated multifractal and the distributed multifractal.

The generalized Hurst exponent of the shuffled liquidity sequence was depicted in Figure 6.4. As indicated in Figure 6.4, after shuffling and resetting the liquidity sequences of the three crude oil futures markets, the value of $h^T(q)$ changed with the value of q, and the $h^T(q) \sim q$ function was a decreasing function, indicating that the shuffled liquidity sequence had multifractal characteristics. Moreover, the value of $h(2)$ was the generalized Hurst exponent obtained by the R/S method. To analyze the sources of the liquidity's multifractality in the crude oil futures markets, we listed the values of $h(2)$ and $h^T(2)$ in Table 6.4. The generalized Hurst exponents of the liquidity sequence before and after the resetting were all larger than 0.5, and $h(2) - h^T(2) \neq 0$. The results showed that the liquidity multifractality of the three crude oil futures was jointly caused by the correlated multifractal and the distributed multifractal.

Table 6.4   Generalized Hurst exponent of two kinds of series

	$h(2)$	$h^T(2)$	$h(2) - h^T(2)$
WTI	0.986	1.047	-0.061
BRENT	0.986	0.787	0.199
INE	0.987	0.909	0.078

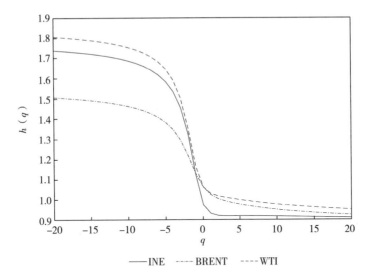

Figure 6. 4   Generalized Hurst exponent of crude oil futures for shuffled data

6. 3. 4   Identification of fluctuation trends

The liquidity of crude oil futures had the multifractal non – linear characteristics.

Based on the multifractal trend identification method, we used the trend entropy di-

mension to identify the fluctuation trend of nonlinear time series. Simultaneously, we

selected 5, 10, 15, 30, 60, 90, and 120 Days as the moving period, and calculated

the liquidity's entropy dimension and trend entropy dimension of WTI, BRENT and

INE crude oil futures during 7 moving periods. The trend entropy dimension divided

the time series into the rising interval and the falling interval. We calculated the en-

tropy dimensions of the time series in the two intervals, respectively. The entropy di-

mensions of different intervals could be classified into the rising entropy dimension

and the falling entropy dimension. Generally, the ordinary entropy dimension does

not distinguish between rising and falling intervals, and the entropy dimension of the entire time series is calculated. Limited by the length of this paper, this section only listed the mean of each dimension. The mean values of the rising entropy dimension of crude oil futures liquidity were listed in Table 6.5, the mean values of the falling entropy dimension of crude oil futures liquidity were listed in Table 6.6, and the mean values of the entropy dimension of crude oil futures liquidity were listed in Table 6.7.

Table 6.5 Mean of rising entropy dimension sequence

	5 Days	10 Days	15 Days	30 Days	60 Days	90 Days	120 Days
WTI	1.084	1.193	1.279	1.337	1.381	1.384	1.436
BRENT	1.073	1.187	1.275	1.339	1.394	1.398	1.449
INE	1.097	1.189	1.257	1.320	1.356	1.387	1.426

Table 6.6 Mean of falling entropy dimension sequence

	5 Days	10 Days	15 Days	30 Days	60 Days	90 Days	120 Days
WTI	1.018	1.188	1.227	1.301	1.333	1.354	1.400
BRENT	1.081	1.193	1.277	1.327	1.365	1.388	1.419
INE	1.074	1.189	1.277	1.313	1.372	1.399	1.425

Table 6.7 Mean of entropy dimension sequence

	5 Days	10 Days	15 Days	30 Days	60 Days	90 Days	120 Days
WTI	1.289	1.292	1.354	1.376	1.415	1.424	1.460
BRENT	1.302	1.302	1.366	1.400	1.439	1.448	1.476
INE	1.303	1.311	1.366	1.388	1.422	1.436	1.470

Judging from the statistical results from Table 6.5 to Table 6.7, during the same moving period, the mean values of the rising entropy dimension, falling entropy dimension and entropy dimension were not equal. Besides, the mean values of the three entropy dimensions generally increased with the extension of the moving period, suggesting that the trend consistency of crude oil futures liquidity was more significant in the short term, while the trend reversion was more significant in the long term. According to the results, there was no trend reversion in the liquidity of crude oil futures, the liquidity of WTI, BRENT and INE crude oil futures market only had the trend consistency that maintained the fluctuation characteristics of the previous time node.

6.3.5　Effectiveness analysis of identification

In the above‑mentioned section, we employed the trend entropy dimension to analyze the fluctuation trend of crude oil futures liquidity. The results showed that the trend consistency of WTI, BRENT and INE crude oil futures liquidity was relatively significant and that there was no trend reversion. The relevant conclusions had certain practical significance and application value. The purpose of this section was to test whether the accuracy of this method would meet the daily needs of investors. Therefore, we needed to further verify the effectiveness of trend entropy dimension in identifying the fluctuation trend of crude oil futures liquidity. We adopted the correct rate of identification to test whether the trend entropy dimension was effective. As the most direct description of the identification effectiveness, the correct rate of identification was the proportion of correct identification times in the total identification times. To avoid data survival bias, this identification method was effective when the correct rate of identification was larger than 0.5.

Table 6.8 denoted the correct rates of identification for three crude oil futures markets. As could be seen from Table 6.8, during different moving periods, the correct rates of identification were all larger than 0.5 in the three crude oil futures mar‑

kets. Specifically, the average identification correct rate of INE crude oil futures liquidity reached 0. 643, and that of WTI and BRENT reached 0. 627 and 0. 647 respectively. During the same moving period, the maximum range of accuracy in the three markets was 0. 036. Therefore, the application of the trend entropy dimension to the identification of the fluctuation trend of crude oil futures liquidity was effective and universal.

Table 6. 8   The correct rate of identification in WTI, BRENT and INE

	5Days	10Days	15Days	30Days	60Days	90Days	120Days
WTI	0. 572	0. 631	0. 634	0. 636	0. 639	0. 638	0. 642
BRENT	0. 587	0. 633	0. 665	0. 672	0. 658	0. 634	0. 677
INE	0. 567	0. 638	0. 654	0. 659	0. 662	0. 656	0. 665

6. 3. 6   Testing of stochastic correct rate

The above results proved that the trend entropy dimension was effective and universal in identifying the fluctuation trend of the liquidity in the three crude oil futures markets. To avoid systematic errors in the identification process, this section would calculate the stochastic correct rate of the trend entropy dimension. Systematic error meant that the number of misidentifications was very small, but the misidentifications were concentrated in a certain time series. This kind of continuous misidentification might cause the result to be unreferenced. Therefore, to avoid such errors, this section improved the statistical method of identification accuracy. We randomly extracted the original time series $\{x_i\}_{i=1}^{N}$, $\{x_{i_t}^{k}\}_{t=1}^{n_k}$ was the sub – sequence extracted from the original time series $\{x_i\}_{i=1}^{N}$, and there were m times of extraction, where $k \in [0,$

$m]$, $n_k \in (2, N]$. For the liquidity's stochastic sequence $\{x_{i_t}^k\}_{t=1}^{n_k}$, we assumed the identification correct rate of trend entropy dimension was p_k, then the stochastic correct rate sequence of the original time series was $\{p_k\}_{k=1}^{m}$. Therefore, if the mean value of the random correct rate sequence $\{p_k\}_{k=1}^{m}$ was significantly larger than 0.5, the trend entropy dimension was effective in identifying the fluctuation trend of the time sequence, and there were no systematic errors in the identification process. During different moving periods, this paper tested the accuracy of crude oil futures liquidity in the three markets. For each test, 100 sets of sub – sequence were randomly selected, and the mean value of the stochastic correct rate was analyzed by T – test. The results were as follows:

Table 6.9　The mean and T – test results of stochastic correct rate sequences

	5 Days	10 Days	15 Days	30 Days	60 Days	90 Days	120 Days
WTI	0.573 *	0.634 *	0.636 *	0.673 **	0.659 *	0.632 *	0.678 *
BRENT	0.588 *	0.631 **	0.665 *	0.635 *	0.640 *	0.636 *	0.643 *
INE	0.568 *	0.640 *	0.655 *	0.658 *	0.664 *	0.655 **	0.669 *

Note: ** indicated significance at the 5% significance level; * indicated significance at the 1% significance level.

In Table 6.9, during whatever moving period, the stochastic correct rate sequences passed the T – test at the significance level of 1% and 5%, and the mean values of the stochastic correct rate sequences for crude oil futures liquidity of the three markets were significantly larger than 0.5. The results showed that the application of trend entropy dimension to the identification of the fluctuation trend of liquidity was effective and did not produce systematic errors. This identification method enjoyed good reference value and universality for the fluctuation trend identification of liquidity.

In summary, whether through the identification accuracy or the T – tests of the stochastic correct rate sequences, the results proved that the trend entropy dimension could more accurately identify the fluctuation trend of crude oil futures liquidity. This method was an effective measurement method of identifying the fluctuation trend of nonlinear time series. For the crude oil futures of WTI, BRENT and INE, the identification accuracy and stochastic accuracy of the three different futures liquidity met the recognition conditions, proving that the trend entropy dimension was robust and universal when identifying the fluctuation trend of crude oil futures liquidity.

6.4   Robustness test

For the test of the multifractal characteristics of crude oil futures liquidity, in the hope of verifying the robustness of the experimental results, we used the Amivest liquidity index of Method 2 and the MF – DFA to analyze the generalized Hurst exponent and calculate the degree of liquidity multifractality in the three crude oil futures markets. Figure 6.5 was the generalized Hurst index of crude oil futures liquidity in three markets. The value of the q – order generalized Hurst index was closely related to the value of q; $h(q)$ was a monotonically decreasing function of q. When $q < 0$, the q value of INE crude oil futures liquidity changed less than that of the other two markets; this result was consistent with the result based on Amihud liquidity index. Furthermore, in Table 6.10, we listed the multifractal degree of crude oil futures liquidity in the three markets, compared and analyzed the multifractal complexity of liquidity. The results proved that the generalized Hurst exponents $h(2)$ of liquidity in the three crude oil futures markets were all larger than 0.5, so the crude oil futures li-quidity had the characteristics of persistence and long – term memory. For the degree of liquidity multifractality, the multifractal degree of INE's crude oil futures liquidity was lower than that of the other two markets, which indicated that the complexity of INE crude oil futures liquidity was lower than that of the other two markets. The calculation result was consistent with the calculation result based on Method 1. Therefore, the application of the MF – DFA to the analysis of the multifractal characteristics of futures liquidity enjoyed good robustness in this paper.

Table 6. 10   The multifractal degree of market liquidity in different markets

	$h(-2)$	$h(2)$	Δh
WTI	1. 368	0. 983	0. 385
BRENT	1. 405	0. 983	0. 422
INE	1. 295	0. 985	0. 309

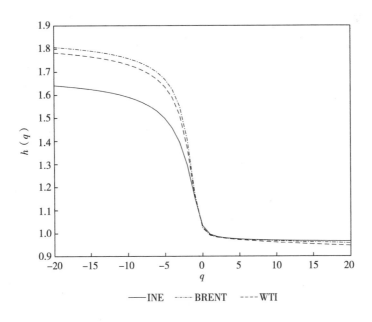

Figure 6. 5   Generalized Hurst exponent of market liquidity in different markets

6.5 Summary

Although the crude oil futures market closed at a negative value, it can be concluded that the value of crude oil futures depends entirely on their liquidity and is significantly affected by liquidity fluctuations. Therefore, whether for the determination of the value of crude oil futures, or for investors and regulators, it is particularly important to study the liquidity fluctuation characteristics of crude oil futures markets and to predict future changes in the liquidity of crude oil futures markets.

To study the liquidity fluctuation characteristics of crude oil futures and predict the fluctuation trend of liquidity, we have used the MF – DFA and the generalized Hurst exponent to analyze the nonlinear characteristics of crude oil futures liquidity and calculate liquidity's multifractal degree and sources of multifractality. According to the non – linear characteristics of crude oil futures liquidity, we have adopted the trend entropy dimension to identify the fluctuation trend of crude oil futures liquidity, test the correct rate of identification and verify the effectiveness of the method by the stochastic correct rate of the trend entropy dimension. Finally, we have conducted a robustness test. We have found that, the liquidity of WTI, BRENT and INE crude oil futures not only has nonlinear characteristics, but also has multifractal characteristics based on the MF – DFA; the generalized Hurst exponent of crude oil futures liquidity changes with the order, which proves that the liquidity of crude oil futures has continuous and long – term memory; the liquidity's multifractal degree of INE crude oil futures is smaller than that of the other two markets, indicating that the complexity of

INE crude oil futures liquidity is also smaller than that of WTI and BRENT crude oil futures; the trend entropy dimension can identify the fluctuation trend of crude oil futures liquidity, and the correct rate of identification and the stochastic correct rate prove the effectiveness and universality of the trend entropy dimension.

The research results of this paper not only have provided a reference for traders' investment decisions and reduced the risks of traders' futures investments, but also have provided suggestions for the relevant authorities to supervise the market risks and extreme risks of the liquidity of crude oil futures. Arguably, the paper can improve the market supervision system and further strengthen the role of crude oil futures markets in avoiding spot market risks.

Chapter 7   The Impact of Liquidity on

Portfolio Selection

7. 1   Introduction

With the rapid economic development and the acceleration of the process of global economic integration, my country's capital market is also constantly developing and improving. Affected by factors such as macroeconomic policies and investor ideology, my country's capital market has changed a lot, and activities such as speculative arbitrage are more frequent. Investors urgently need the guidance of relevant investment theories in order to conduct rational investment activities. At the same time, with the rapid development of computer and communication technology and its wide application in the financial market, the risks and influence of the financial market are increasing day by day. In – depth study of modern investment portfolio theory has important practical significance.

Investment portfolio selection refers to how investors can effectively and reasonably allocate various financial assets in the face of uncertainty, so as to satisfy investors' balance of risks and returns. As the basis of modern portfolio theory, Markowitz assumed that investors are risk – averse in 1952, and used the mean and variance of returns to express expected returns and risks, respectively, discussed the selection of the optimal asset portfolio under uncertain conditions, and established the mean – variance portfolio selection model. The mean – variance model of asset portfolio is the cornerstone of modern portfolio theory and the cornerstone of the entire modern financial theory.

The mean – variance model assumes that the market is frictionless and does not consider the impact of transaction costs on portfolio selection. In fact, in the process of implementing investment portfolios, due to the large differences in transaction costs of different trading strategies, ignoring transaction costs may often lead to invalid asset portfolios. Therefore, investors need to consider the impact of trading strategies on the construction of investment portfolios when constructing investment portfolios. At the same time, in the actual securities market, investors seldom only carry out one – stage investment activities. It is very important to adjust the investment portfolio in a timely and effective manner in accordance with the continuous changes in the market environment. Mossin (1968) extended the Markowitz single – stage model to the multi – stage case. Subsequently, Merton (1969), Chen et al. (1971), Hakansson (1971), Elton and Gruber (1974), Dumas and Luciano (1991), Zhu (2004) et al. conducted an in – depth discussion on the problem of multi – stage portfolio selection, and proposed a multi – stage portfolio selection model and algorithm. Dantzig et al. (1993), Consigh (1998) use a multi – stage stochastic programming model to solve the problem of dynamic portfolio selection. However, it is very difficult to solve the dynamic mean – variance portfolio selection model. Li and Ng (2007) simplified the multi – stage mean – variance portfolio selection problem to a problem that can be handled by dynamic programming, and obtained an analytical formula of effective frontier portfolio.

To sum up, many scholars have studied the problem of portfolio selection, but most of them consider a given transaction cost function and analyze its impact on investor portfolio selection. They did not combine the selection of investment portfolio with the formulation of algorithmic trading strategies for research. Because the transaction costs of different algorithmic trading strategies are very different and have a very important impact on the selection of investment portfolios, this chapter combines the design of algorithmic trading strategies with the selection of investment portfolios for analysis, and consider the problem of portfolio selection based on the optimal trading strategy.

7.2　Portfolio selection and liquidity cost

7.2.1　Portfolio selection

The modern portfolio theory was first proposed by the American economist Harry Markowitz in 1952 in the article "Securities Portfolio Selection". The rate of return of securities is regarded as a random variable, and the mean value of this random variable is used to represent the return of the portfolio, and this random variable is used. The standard deviation of represents the risk of the portfolio. Therefore, the problem of portfolio securities selection can be reduced to solving an appropriate investment ratio in order to make the investment portfolio return to a given mean value and the smallest variance mathematical programming problem, this problem is called the mean – variance model. The application of this model allows investors to quantify risks, creating a precedent for modern financial theories and investment analysis theories. From now on, finance is no longer a purely descriptive and qualitative research based on empirical operations, and begins to use quantitative methods to study financial issues.

Markowitz pioneered the theory and method of asset portfolio investment by rational investors under uncertain conditions. For the first time, he used quantitative methods to analyze the advantages of investors in diversified investment, and proposed a view that investors who enjoy high returns must bear high risks. The model is obtained under many assumptions, mainly:

(1) The utility function of investors is increasing, that is to say, the attitude towards returns is the more the better, the pursuit of maximum returns under a certain level of risk, or the pursuit of minimum risk under a certain level of income;

(2) The utility function of investors is diminishing, which means that investors are risk averse;

(3) The rate of return of risky assets obeys a normal distribution;

(4) There is no transaction cost.

Among the asset portfolios with the same rate of return, the asset portfolio with the smallest variance is called the frontier asset portfolio. For the asset portfolio p, if it is a frontier asset portfolio, then if and only if the n dimensional asset portfolio weight vector w_p is the solution to the following mathematical programming problem (Markowitz, 1952).

$$\min_{\{w\}} \frac{1}{2} w^T V w \tag{7.1}$$

$$\text{s. t. } w^T e - w^T \beta = E[\tilde{r}_p] \tag{7.1a}$$

$$w^T I = 1 \tag{7.1b}$$

Among them, V represents the covariance matrix of the n assets; e is a n dimensional vector used to represent the expected rate of return of this n assets; $E[\tilde{r}_p]$ is the expected rate of return of the asset portfolio; I represents the unit vector of the n dimension.

The objective function of the model (7.1) is to minimize the variance $w^T V w$ of the asset portfolio under a given expected rate of return $E[\tilde{r}_p]$; the constraint condition (7.1a) represents the expected rate of return $E[\tilde{r}_p]$ of the asset portfolio; the constraint condition (7.1b) Indicates that the sum of the weights of the asset portfolio is 1.

The mathematical programming model (7.1) can be solved using the Lagrangian method, and the portfolio weight vector w_p is the solution to the following problems:

$$\min_{\{w, \lambda, \gamma\}} L = \frac{1}{2} w^T V w + \lambda (E[\tilde{r}_p] - w^T e) + \gamma (1 - w^T I) \tag{7.2}$$

Among them, λ and γ is two positive constants. The first – order conditions of the above model are:

$$\frac{\partial L}{\partial x_0} = V w_p - \lambda e - \gamma I = 0 \tag{7.3}$$

$$\frac{\partial L}{\partial \lambda} = E(\tilde{r}_p) - w^T e = 0 \tag{7.4}$$

$$\frac{\partial L}{\partial \gamma} = 1 - w^T I = 0 \tag{7.5}$$

Solving the above equations with (7.1a) and (7.1b) together can get:

$$\lambda = \frac{CE[\tilde{r}_p] - A}{D} \qquad\qquad (7.6)$$

$$\gamma = \frac{B - AE[\tilde{r}_p]}{D} \qquad\qquad (7.7)$$

Among them,

$$A = I^T V^{-1} e \qquad\qquad (7.8)$$

$$B = e^T V^{-1} e \qquad\qquad (7.9)$$

$$C = I^T V^{-1} I \qquad\qquad (7.10)$$

$$D = BC - A^2 \qquad\qquad (7.11)$$

Substituting formula (7.6) and formula (7.7) into formula (7.3) can be obtained,

$$w_p = g + hE[\tilde{r}_p] \qquad\qquad (7.12)$$

Among them,

$$g = \frac{BV^{-1}I - AV^{-1}e}{D} \qquad\qquad (7.13)$$

$$h = \frac{CV^{-1}e - AV^{-1}I}{D} \qquad\qquad (7.14)$$

7.2.2   Liquidity cost

For the liquidity cost, investors cannot accurately estimate before the transaction, and cannot accurately measure it after the transaction, which is more difficult to estimate. However, through the "iceberg" model of Plexus, it can be seen that liquidity cost is one of the most important components of investor transaction costs and reflects the complex connection between transaction, price and information. It is also known as the market shocks or price shocks cost.

Price shock refers to the change in the price of a security caused by an investor's order after it is submitted to the market for execution. Its size can be measured by the difference between the execution price of the order and the price of the security when the order does not exist in the security market. In the actual securities trading process, investors cannot directly observe these two prices at the same time, so many scholars have proposed different methods for estimating the cost of price shocks. Brown et al. (1988), Easterwood and Nutt (1999), Krinsky and Lee (1996), etc. believe that price shock is a linear function of transaction volume or transaction speed, that is, the price shock cost of investors in the entire transaction process can be expressed as:

$$PI = \beta x \tag{7.15}$$

Among them, PI represents the price shock cost, β is a constant greater than zero, x represents the investor's order size or transaction speed.

When the informational market conveyed in an investor's order changes the company's long – term growth potential, other market participants will quickly adjust the stock price to a new reasonable level after learning some information, and these activities will affect the future expectations of the stock price, causing the intrinsic value of the stock to change, then this shock is a permanent price shock. Permanent price shocks are caused by the information conveyed by investors' orders, so many scholars agree that permanent price shocks are a linear function of transaction volume or transaction speed.

If an investor's order is submitted to the securities market, the information conveyed by the order does not change the intrinsic value of the stock, but is only caused by a temporary imbalance between supply and demand, then the price impact of the order on the market at this time is a temporary price impact. Such temporary shocks are usually relatively short – lived. They are price shocks caused by imbalances in timeliness requirements and short – term liquidity demands. They will not affect the intrinsic value of stocks, and the stock prices will return to the original expected price level in a short time. Temporary price shocks are price changes caused by investor's timeliness requirements or short – term liquidity requirements. Such changes are closely related to factors such as transaction volume, transaction time, order type, market liquidity, etc. Therefore, Kissell and Glantz (2003) believes that temporary price shocks should be a non – linear function of factors such as transaction volume. The specific estimation method is as follows.

Suppose an investor plans to use a phased algorithmic trading strategy $y = (y_1, y_2, \cdots, y_m)'$ to trade a total amount of S securities in the next m trading period. A-mong them, y_t indicates the size of the order that investors are prepared to submit during the period t. The price shock cost for investors using this trading strategy is:

$$PI(y) = \sum_{t=1}^{m} y_t \left[\frac{\alpha I y_t}{(y_t + 0.5v_t)S} + \frac{(1-\alpha)I}{S} \right] \tag{7.16}$$

Among them, v_t represents the market transaction volume during the expected period, $t = 1, 2, \cdots, m$; S represents the total order size during the entire trading period, namely: $S = \sum_{t=1}^{m} y_t$; I represents the instantaneous shock cost; α represents the temporary price shock ratio.

7.3   Portfolio selection based on the linear liquidity cost

Assuming that the liquidity cost is a linear function of the transaction volume, since the liquidity cost is only related to the investor's transaction volume at this time, and has nothing to do with which trading strategy the investor adopts, it may be assumed that the liquidity cost (price shock cost) function is:

$$PI_k = \beta_k x_k (k = 1, 2, \cdots, n) \qquad (7.17)$$

Among them, β_k is the price shock coefficient.

$$\min \frac{1}{2} x^T V x \qquad (7.18)$$

$$\text{s. t. } x^T e - x^T \beta = E[\tilde{r}_p] \qquad (7.18a)$$

$$x^T P = R \qquad (7.18b)$$

Among them, e is the expected return rate vector of the assets invested by the investor; $E[\tilde{r}_p]$ represents the expected return rate of the asset portfolio; P represents the price vector of the asset portfolio; R represents the investor's total capital holdings.

According to the Lagrangian method, x_0 is the optimal solution of the following formula:

$$\min_{\{x, \lambda, \gamma\}} L = \frac{1}{2} x_0^T V x_0 + \lambda (E[\tilde{r}_p] - x_0^T e + x_0^T \beta) + \gamma (R - x_0^T P) \qquad (7.19)$$

Among them, λ and γ is two positive constants.

The first - order optimality conditions of the model (7.19) are:

$$\frac{\partial L}{\partial x_0} = V x_0 - \lambda e + \lambda \beta - \gamma 1 = 0 \qquad (7.20)$$

$$\frac{\partial L}{\partial \lambda} = E(\tilde{r}_p) - x_0^T e + x_0^T \beta = 0 \qquad (7.21)$$

$$\frac{\partial L}{\partial \gamma} = R - x_0^T p = 0 \qquad (7.22)$$

Solving the above formulas together with formulas (7.18a) and (7.18b) can be obtained:

$$x = \left[\frac{R}{A(AD - BC)} - \frac{B(AE(\tilde{r}_p) - RC)}{A(AD - BC)}\right](V^{-1}e - V'\beta) + \frac{AE(\tilde{r}_p) - RC}{AD - BC}V'\beta$$

$$(7.23)$$

Among them,

$$A = P^T V^{-1} e - P^T V^{-1} \beta \qquad\qquad (7.24)$$

$$B = P^T V^{-1} \beta \qquad\qquad (7.25)$$

$$C = e^T V^{-1} e - e^T V^{-1} \beta - \beta^T V^{-1} e + \beta^T V^{-1} \beta \qquad\qquad (7.26)$$

$$D = e^T V^{-1} \beta - \beta^T V^{-1} \beta \qquad\qquad (7.27)$$

7. 4　Portfolio selection based on the nonlinear liquidity cost

　　If the liquidity cost is a non − linear function of investor trading volume, then this liquidity cost function is not easy to determine. Therefore, this study uses Kissell and Glantz (2003) to propose a method for estimating price shocks to measure the liquidity cost in this study. The investor price shock cost function can be expressed as:

$$PI(y) = \sum_{t=1}^{m} y_t \left[\frac{\alpha I y_t}{(y_t + 0.5 v_t)S} + \frac{(1 - \alpha)I}{S}\right] \qquad\qquad (7.28)$$

　　Among them, m represents the number of trading periods; v_t represents the market volume during the expected period; y_t represents the order size during the period t; S represents the total order size during the entire trading period, namely: $S = \sum_{t=1}^{m} y_t$; I represents the instantaneous impact cost; α represents the temporary price impact ratio.

The problem of optimal trading strategy when investors only consider price shock costs can be described by the following model:

$$minPI(y) = \sum_{t=1}^{m} y_t \left[\frac{\alpha I y_t}{(y_t + 0.5v_t)S} + \frac{(1-\alpha)I}{S} \right] \qquad (7.29)$$

$$s.\ t.\ S = \sum_{t=1}^{m} y_t \qquad (7.29a)$$

$$y_t \geqslant 0,\ t = 1,\ 2,\ \cdots,\ m \qquad (7.29b)$$

The optimal solution to this problem is:

$$y_t = S \frac{v_t}{V},\ t = 1,\ 2,\ \cdots,\ m \qquad (7.30)$$

Obviously, the optimal trading strategy when investors only consider the cost of price shocks is the volume – weighted average price trading strategy (VWAP). At this time, the total price shock cost of investors is:

$$PI(S) = \frac{\alpha IS}{S + 0.5V} + (1-\alpha)I \qquad (7.31)$$

The investor's portfolio selection model can be expressed by the following mathematical programming model:

$$\min \frac{1}{2} R^2 \sum_{i=1}^{n} \sum_{i=1}^{n} x_i x_j \sigma_{ij} \qquad (7.32)$$

$$s.\ t.\ \sum_{i=1}^{n} Rx_i E(\tilde{r}_i) - \sum_{i=1}^{n} PI_i(x_i) \geqslant Rr_p \qquad (7.32a)$$

$$\sum_{i=1}^{n} x_i = 1 \qquad (7.32b)$$

$$0 \leqslant x_i \leqslant 1 (i = 1,\ 2,\ \cdots,\ n) \qquad (7.32c)$$

Among them, x_i is the proportion of funds invested by investors in securities i; $E[\tilde{r}_i]$ is the expected rate of return of the securities i; $E[\tilde{r}_p]$ represents the expected rate of return of the asset portfolio; P represents the price vector of the asset portfolio; R represents the investor's capital holdings.

Since the above portfolio selection model based on the cost of nonlinear price shocks is too complicated to obtain an analytical solution, numerical examples will be used for analysis below. This study randomly selects 10 stocks in the Shenzhen A - share market, as shown in Table 7. 1. Assume that the expected return of the investment portfolio constructed by the investor is $r_p = 0.0002$, and the investor's capital holdings are $R = 1$, 000, 000.

Table 7. 1   Sample stock names

Stock code	Stock name	Trading Days (Days)	Market type
000004	National Agriculture Technology	233	Shenzhen A shares
000009	Baoan, China	234	Shenzhen A shares
000011	Shenzhen Property A	238	Shenzhen A shares
000016	Deep Konka A	238	Shenzhen A shares
000018	Crown A	237	Shenzhen A shares
000025	Teli A	238	Shenzhen A shares
000078	Aquaman Bio	236	Shenzhen A shares
000151	Zhongcheng shares	238	Shenzhen A shares
000153	Fengyuan Pharmaceutical	228	Shenzhen A shares
000591	Tongjun Court	236	Shenzhen A shares

This study uses the relevant transaction data of my country's Shenzhen Stock Exchange from January 1, 2013 to December 31, 2013 to compare and analyze the total income of investors when they adjust their investment portfolio once a year, half a year, a quarter, or two months. Table 7. 2 shows the investment ratio, income, and cost of each stock in the portfolio under different adjustment frequencies. Table 7. 3 shows the prices of stocks in different periods. The prices in this table are mainly the

Table 7.2　Each stock in the portfolio under different adjustment frequencies

	a year	6 months		3 months				2 months					
		1	2	1	2	3	4	1	2	3	4	5	6
000004	0.0134	0.0123	0.1605	0.0242	0.0061	0.1353	0.2012	0.1344	0.0030	0.0984	0.1130	0.0148	0.0424
000009	0.0001	0.1353	0.0689	0.0109	0.1621	0.0333	0.1243	0.0627	0.4469	0.1875	0.2187	0.0517	0.4019
000011	0.0299	0.0569	0.0636	0.3095	0.4827	0.0912	0.0194	0.1465	0.0034	0.0354	0.5911	0.0873	0.0331
000016	0.1456	0.0126	0.0000	0.1215	0.0000	0.0129	0.0592	0.2657	0.0624	0.2128	0.0000	0.1183	0.0979
000018	0.2707	0.0754	0.2758	0.0124	0.1171	0.4822	0.0328	0.0674	0.0618	0.0167	0.0295	0.0130	0.0180
000025	0.0433	0.0742	0.2285	0.0731	0.0249	0.0201	0.0465	0.0712	0.0633	0.1158	0.0028	0.1832	0.0077
000078	0.0275	0.0000	0.0540	0.1474	0.0461	0.1192	0.1275	0.1330	0.0785	0.1598	0.0000	0.1423	0.2758
000151	0.0298	0.2885	0.0200	0.0323	0.0848	0.0618	0.0246	0.0000	0.1466	0.0510	0.0203	0.1742	0.0241
000153	0.2626	0.1999	0.0596	0.2537	0.0191	0.0168	0.1160	0.0091	0.1323	0.0393	0.0000	0.0912	0.0150
000591	0.1771	0.1451	0.0690	0.0151	0.0591	0.0274	0.2485	0.1152	0.0018	0.0832	0.0294	0.1239	0.0842
Income	1,813,100	631,000	1,253,000	852,320	872,460	1,419,800	−733,860	800,700	494,490	407,000	811,650	64,829	−143,990
Cost	153,660	116,724	147,032	105,410	108,816	198,488	91,924	111,454	91,620	97,834	87,912	86,212	85,674
Profit	1,659,440	514,276	1,105,968	746,910	763,644	1,221,312	−825,784	689,246	402,870	309,166	723,738	−21,383	−229,664

stock prices and ending prices when investors adjust their investment portfolio each time; Therefore, combining the amount of funds invested in different stocks by investors in each adjustment of the investment portfolio in Table 7.2, we can get the investor's profit during the holding period of the investment portfolio. For the situation where the investment portfolio is adjusted every six months, every quarter, and every two months, the total profit of the investor is equal to the sum of the profit after each adjustment.

Table 7.3   Prices of the sample stocks in different periods

	2012. 12	2013. 02	2013. 03	2013. 04	2013. 06	2013. 08	2013. 10	2013. 12
000004	8. 18	10. 05	9. 54	10. 64	10. 00	12. 16	11. 67	11. 65
000009	8. 80	9. 11	9. 96	9. 92	11. 00	9. 92	9. 86	9. 45
000011	7. 19	7. 10	6. 17	7. 39	7. 93	9. 07	7. 91	7. 81
000016	3. 16	3. 44	3. 16	3. 41	3. 41	3. 52	3. 79	3. 86
000018	6. 69	7. 62	8. 52	7. 77	8. 83	9. 83	8. 90	9. 57
000025	6. 15	6. 75	6. 18	6. 03	6. 03	6. 61	6. 95	8. 78
000078	5. 82	7. 88	7. 26	7. 41	7. 41	6. 71	7. 40	7. 55
000151	6. 86	7. 42	8. 08	8. 05	8. 05	7. 75	7. 35	7. 30
000153	6. 48	7. 26	7. 82	8. 12	8. 12	7. 47	7. 39	7. 82
000591	6. 29	7. 03	6. 82	6. 31	7. 17	8. 27	8. 86	8. 21

Note: Stock prices are all closing prices on the last trading day of the corresponding month.

Figure 7.1 shows the total profit and transaction cost of investors under different investment portfolio adjustment intervals. It can be seen from Figure 7.1 that as the frequency of investor's investment in adjusting their portfolios increases within a year, investor's total income, transaction costs, and total profits also increase; The impact of algorithmic trading strategies on the portfolio is mainly reflected by transaction costs. After considering the impact of algorithmic trading strategies, the more frequent the portfolio adjustment, the greater the transaction cost, and as the frequency of adjustment increases, the marginal growth rate relative to the total investor income, the marginal growth rate of transaction costs is greater. By comparing and analyzing the total income of investors when they adjust their investment portfolios every year, every six months, every quarter, and every two months, it can be known that the total profit of investors is the largest when they are adjusted every quarter.

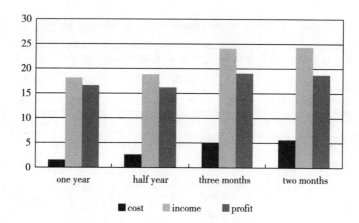

Figure 7.1   Investors' investment income and costs at different adjustment intervals

Note: The abscissa represents the time interval for investors to adjust the investment portfolio once, and the unit of ordinate is 100, 000 yuan.

7. 5   Summary

In the actual securities market, investors face the impact of various transaction costs in the process of implementing investment portfolios. This chapter combines the design of algorithmic trading strategy and the problem of portfolio selection for analysis, and considers the impact of different adjustment frequencies of investment portfolios on investment income under the influence of algorithmic trading strategies. The results of the research show that, compared with adjusting the investment portfolio every year, every six months, and every two months, investors make the most profit when they adjust their investment portfolio every quarter. At this time, the investment income is relatively large, and the relative adjustments are more frequent. The transaction cost at this time is also small. In summary, taking into account the influence of algorithmic trading strategies during the execution of the investment process, investors' portfolio adjustments are not as frequent as possible. It is necessary to integrate factors such as expected returns, risks and transaction costs of stocks. The investment portfolio model under consideration of algorithmic trading strategies and the optimal adjustment frequency of the investment portfolio proposed in this chapter provide a certain theoretical basis for investors to construct a reasonable investment portfolio.

Conclusions

Liquidity is an important indicator of the quality of financial market development. Existing researches on liquidity are mainly in the areas of the impact of liquidity on asset pricing and the relationship between liquidity and investor behavior, but there are few studies on the characteristics of liquidity itself. In fact, the prediction of the future trend of liquidity is particularly important. For investors, if they can accurately determine the changes in liquidity in advance, they can adjust their investment strategies in a targeted and timely manner, reduce transaction costs, and increase investment returns. In other words, if you have a more accurate judgment on the future changes in liquidity, you can intervene in time before extreme volatility occurs in the market to avoid extreme volatility. In order to accurately predict the future trend of liquidity, we must understand and master the characteristics of liquidity, especially volatility. Based on the current development of my country's financial market, this book first proposes liquidity measurement methods, analyzes the influencing factors of liquidity, and uses methods such as multifractal theory, generalized Hurst index, and trend entropy dimension to study China's new third board market and the market. The volatility characteristics of liquidity in the stock market, stock index futures market, and energy futures market; subsequently, the use of multifractal – detrend volatility analysis method to study the volatility characteristics of market liquidity in China's securities market, stock index futures market, etc. ; finally, the use of trend entropy dimensions, etc. Models and methods predict these market liquidity fluctuation trends, and prove the accuracy and effectiveness of the prediction method.

Firstly, we use the method of Kyle (1985) and Chiyachantana et al. (2004) to estimate market shocks of sample securities, theoretically analyze the relationship between market shocks and stock price changes, and study the impact of market shocks on stock price changes. At the same time, based on the historical high – frequency trading data of China's security market, the scale of market shocks is estimated, and the trading day is divided into eight different trading periods, and analyze the impact of the circulation market value, turnover rate and order size on market shocks. The results show that although the market shock is an extra cost for investors, it has both disadvantages and advantages for the whole security market. For investors, if the stock price is in a rising stage and the order is executed at this time, market shocks will increase the price of the stock. If the stock price is in a declining stage and the order is executed at this time, market shocks will slow down the decline of the stock price, make the stock price changes tend to moderation, and reduce the volatility of the security market. The turnover rate is a significant factor affecting market shocks, while the circulation market value, which is more concerned by investors, has no significant impact on market shocks. For large – cap stocks with a smaller turnover rate, although the circulation market value is large, the total transaction amount is relatively smaller, so the market shock is greater, and the stock price is also vulnerable to the impact of large orders. Therefore, no matter for ordinary investors or institutional investors, they should pay much attention on stocks with a higher turnover rate in the investment process. For the regulators, they should focus on large‐cap stocks with less liquidity in order to prevent the stock market price from dramatic fluctuations.

Secondly, we investigate the nonlinear feature of market liquidity in China's new OTC market. We select 990 listed companies in the new OTC market as a sample, use the MF‐DFA method and the generalized Hurst exponent to analyze the liquidity's nonlinear feature, compare the multifractal degree of market liquidity in the new OTC market and the large‐cap market. Meanwhile, to analyze the sources of market liquidity's non‐linear in the new OTC market, we reset the liquidity time series to analyze the nonlinear feature, select 10 stocks in the new OTC market to identify the liquidity trended fluctuations by trend entropy dimension. We carry out the robustness test. The results show that the market liquidity of the new OTC market is multifractal and the generalized Hurst exponent of market liquidity is related to the change of order; The liquidity multifractal degree of the new OTC market is lower than that of the large‐cap market, which indicates that the complexity of market liquidity in the new OTC market is lower; The trend entropy dimension is validity and universality in identifying trended fluctuations of market liquidity.

Thirdly, we use the improved Amihud liquidity index to measure the liquidity of CSI300 index futures. According to the holding period of futures contracts, it is divided into four kinds of contracts: current month contract, next month contract, inter season contract and next season contract. The sample range is from April 16, 2010 to December 31, 2019. Based on the nonlinear characteristics of the financial market, this paper analyzes the nonlinear characteristics of futures liquidity and the degree and causes of multifractality by using MF‐DFA and generalized Hurst exponent. In addition, combined with the non‐linear characteristics of futures liquidity, this paper uses the trendency entropy dimension method to recognize the fluctuation trend of futures liquidity, and detects the accuracy of the trendency entropy dimension to recognize liquidity under seven moving periods. In order to avoid systematic error, this paper uses random correct rate to verify the effectiveness of the method. Finally, the robustness test is carried out. The results show that: MF – DFA verifies that the liquidity of CSI 300 index futures not only has nonlinear characteristics, but also has multifractal characteristics; The value of generalized Hurst exponent changes with the order, and the value of four futures contracts liquidity ranges from 0.5 to 1, which proves that the liquidity of futures has nonlinear characteristics of persistence and long – term memory; According to the average daily trading volume of futures contracts, the shorter the holding period, the larger the average daily trading volume of futures contracts. Frequent market transactions of investors increase the complexity of liquidity fluctuation, and increase the market risk and extreme risk of futures liquidity. Therefore, the regulatory authorities need to focus on strengthening the supervision of short – term contract transactions, and pay attention to the liquidity changes of long – term contracts; The trend entropy dimension can recognize the fluctuation trend of futures liquidity in different stages, and the recognition correct rate and random correct rate test prove the effectiveness and universality of this method.

At last, we have used the MF – DFA and the generalized Hurst exponent to analyze the nonlinear characteristics of crude oil futures liquidity and calculate liquidity's multifractal degree and sources of multifractality. According to the non – linear characteristics of crude oil futures liquidity, we have adopted the trend entropy dimension to identify the fluctuation trend of crude oil futures liquidity, test the correct rate of identification and verify the effectiveness of the method by the stochastic correct rate of the trend entropy dimension. Finally, we have conducted a robustness test. The results show that the liquidity of WTI, BRENT and INE crude oil futures not only has nonlinear characteristics, but also has multifractal characteristics based on the MF – DFA; the generalized Hurst exponent of crude oil futures liquidity changes with the order, which proves that the liquidity of crude oil futures has continuous and long – term memory; the liquidity's multifractal degree of INE crude oil futures is smaller than that of the other two markets, indicating that the complexity of INE crude oil futures liquidity is also smaller than that of WTI and BRENT crude oil futures; the trend entropy dimension can identify the fluctuation trend of crude oil futures liquidity, and the correct rate of identification and the stochastic correct rate prove the effectiveness and universality of the trend entropy dimension.

References

[1] Adam K. , Marcet A. , Nicolini J. P. Stock market volatility and learning [J] . The Journal of Finance, 2016, 71 (1): 33 – 82.

[2] Almgren R. , C. Thum, E. Hatptmann. Equity market impact [J] . Journal of Risk, 2005, 18 (7): 57 – 62.

[3] Alzahrani A. A. , Gregoriou A. , Hudson R. Price impact of block trades in the saudi stock market [J] . Journal of International Financial Markets, Institutions and Money, 2012, 23 (2): 322 – 341.

[4] Amihud Y. Illiquidity and stock returns: Cross – section and time – series effects [J] . Journal of Financial Markets, 2002 (1) .

[5] Barclay M. J. , Warner J. B. Stealth trading and volatility: Which trades move prices? [J] . Journal of Financial Economics, 1993, 34 (3): 281 – 305.

[6] Berkowitz A. S. , Logue E. D. The total cost of transactions on the NYSE [J] . Journal of Finance, 1988, 43 (1): 97 – 112.

[7] Bernstein R. The earning expectation life cycle [J] . Financial Analysts Journal, 1993, 49 (2): 90 – 93.

[8] Black F. Toward a fully automated stock exchange [J] . Financial Analysts Journal, 1971 (4) .

[9] Blum G. A. , Kracaw W. A. , Lewellen W. G. Determinants of the execution costs of common stock trades by individual investors [J]. Journal of Financial Research, 1986, 9 (4): 291 – 301.

[10] Borio C. Market distress and vanishing liquidity: Anatomy and policy options [R]. Working Paper, 2004.

[11] Brunnermeier M. K. , Pedersen L. H. Market liquidity and funding liquidity [J]. Review of Financial Studies, 2009, 22 (6): 2201 – 2238.

[12] Peng C. K. , Buldyrev S. V. , Havlin S. , et al. Mosaic organization of DNA nucleotides [J]. Phys. Rev. E. , 1994 (49): 1685 – 1689.

[13] Chiyachantana C. N. , Jain P. K. , Jiang C. , et al. International evidence on institutional trading behavior and price impact [J]. The Journal of Finance, 2004, 59 (2): 869 – 898.

[14] Cont R. , A. Kukanov, S. Stoikov. The price impact of order book events [J]. Journal of Financial Econometrics, 2013, 12 (1): 47 – 88.

[15] Danlei Gu, Jingjing Huang. Multifractal detrended fluctuation analysis on high – frequency SZSE in Chinese stock market [J]. Physica A. , 2019 (521): 225 – 235.

[16] DeBondt W. F. M. , Thaler R. Does the stock market overreact? [J]. The Journal of Finance, 1985, 40 (3): 793 – 805.

[17] Domowitz I. , Glen J. , Madhavan A. Liquidity, volatility and equity trading costs across countries and over time [J]. International Finance, 2001, 4 (2): 221 – 255.

[18] Doyne Farmer J. , L. S. Gillemot, F. Lillo, et al. What really causes large price changes? [J]. Quantitative Finance, 2004, 4 (4): 383 – 397.

[19] Eisler Z. , J. P. Bouchaud, J. Kockelkoren. The price impact of order

book events: Market orders, limit orders and cancellations [J] . Quantitative Finance, 2012, 12 (9): 1395 – 1419.

[20] Falconer K. Fractal geometry (2nd Edition) [M] . Chichester: John Wiley & Sons, Inc. , 2003.

[21] Foster F. D. , Viswanathan S. Variations in trading volume, return volatility, and trading costs: Evidence on recent price formation models [J] . The Journal of Finance, 1993, 48 (1): 187 – 211.

[22] Galariotis E. C. Contrarian and momentum trading: A review of the literature [J] . Review of Behavioral Finance, 2014, 6 (1): 63 – 82.

[23] Glosten L. R. , Harris L. E. Estimating the components of the bid/ask spread [J] . Journal of Financial Economics, 1988, 21 (1): 123 – 142.

[24] Hasbrouck J. , R. A. Schwartz. Liquidity and execution costs in equity markets [J] . The Journal of Portfolio Management, 1988, 14 (3): 10 – 16.

[25] Hasbrouck Joel. Intraday price formation in U. S. equity index markets [J] . Journal of Finance, 2003, 58 (6): 2375 – 2400.

[26] Hu G. Measures of implicit trading costs and buy – sell asymmetry [J] . Journal of Financial Markets, 2009, 12 (3): 418 – 437.

[27] Huberman G. , W. Stanzl. Price Manipulation and quasi – arbitrage [J] . Econometrica, 2004, 72 (4): 1247 – 1275.

[28] J. W. Kantelhardt, S. A. Zschiegner, E. Koscielny – Bunde, S. Havlin, A. Bunde, H. E. Stanley. Multifractal detrended fluctuation analysis of nonstationary time series [J] . Physica A. , 2002 (316): 87 – 114.

[29] Jegadeesh N. , Titman S. Returns to buying winners and selling losers: Implications for stock market efficiency [J] . The Journal of Finance, 1993, 48 (1): 65 – 91.

[30] Jianxin Wang. Liquidity commonality among Asian equity markets [J]. Pacific – Basin Finance Journal, 2013 (21): 1209 – 1231.

[31] Keim D. B., A. Madhavan. Transactions costs and investment style: An inter – exchange analysis of institutional equity trades [J]. Journal of Financial Economics, 1997, 46 (3): 265 – 292.

[32] Kissell R., Glantz M. Optimal trading strategies: Quantitative approaches for managing market impact and trading risk [M]. New York: Amacom, 2003.

[33] Kissell R., Malamut R. Algorithmic decision – making framework [J]. The Journal of Trading, 2006, 1 (1): 12 – 21.

[34] Kissell R., M. Glantz. Optimal trading strategies quantitative approaches for managing market impact and trading risk [M]. New York: Amacom, 2003.

[35] Kissell R., M. Glantz, R. Malamut. A practical framework for estimating transaction costs and developing optimal trading strategies to achieve best execution [J]. Finance Research Letters, 2004, 1 (1): 35 – 46.

[36] Kogan L., S. A. Ross, J. Wang, et al. The price impact and survival of irrational traders [J]. The Journal of Finance, 2006, 61 (1): 195 – 229.

[37] Kyle A. S. Continuous auctions and insider trading [J]. Econometrica, 1985, 53 (6): 1315 – 1335.

[38] Lillo F., Farmer J. D., Mantegna R. N. Master curve for price – impact function [J]. Nature, 2003, 421 (9): 129 – 130.

[39] Loderer C., W. J. Cooney, D. L. Van Drunen. The price elasticity of demand for common stock [J]. Journal of Finance, 1991, 46 (2): 621 – 651.

[40] M. Münnix, T. Shimada, R. Schäfer. Identifying states of a financial market [J]. Sci. Rep., 2012 (2): 644 – 647.

[41] Malinova K., A. Park. Liquidity, volume and price efficiency: The im-

pact of order vs. quote driven trading [J] . Journal of Financial Markets, 2013, 16 (1): 104 – 126.

[42] Mandelbrot B. B. A multifractal walk down wall street [J] . Scientific American, 1999, 280 (2): 70 – 73.

[43] Pastor L. , Stambaugh R. Liquidity risk and expected stock returns [J] . Journal of Political Economy, 2003 (3): 642 – 685.

[44] R. Gu, W. Xiong, X. Li. Does the singular value decomposition entropy have predictive power for stock market? Evidence from the Shenzhen stock market [J] . Physica A. , 2015 (439): 103 – 113.

[45] Ren F. , L. X. Zhong. The price impact asymmetry of institutional trading in the Chinese stock market [J] . Physica A: Statistical Mechanics and Its Applications, 2012, 391 (8): 2667 – 2677.

[46] Ryu D. Price impact asymmetry of futures trades: Trade direction and trade size [J] . Emerging Markets Review, 2013 (14): 110 – 130.

[47] Terrence H. , C. M. Jones, A. J. Menkveld. Does algorithmic trading improve liquidity? [J] . Journal of Finance, 2011, 66 (1): 1 – 33.

[48] Wagner W. H. , Edwards M. Best execution [J] . Financial Analysts Journal, 1993 (49): 65 – 71.

[49] X. Wu, W. Chun, Y. Lin, Y. Li. Identification of momentum life cycle stage of stock price [J] . Nonlinear Dynamics, 2018 (94): 249 – 260.

[50] Y. Amihud, Haim Mendelson. Asset pricing and the bid – ask spread [J] . Journal of Financial Economics, 1986, 17 (2): 223 – 249.

[51] Y. Wei, Y. Wang, D. Huang. A copula – multifractal volatility hedging model for CSI 300 index futures [J] . Physica A. , 2011 (390): 4260 – 4272.